POEMS TO ENJOY: BOOK THREE

Chosen and Edited by Verner Bickley

5th Edition

Proverse Hong Kong

VERNER BICKLEY, MBE, PhD, is a well-known "voice", educationist, and adjudicator, who has held director-level positions in Universities and Government Departments. He is Chairman Emeritus of the English-Speaking Union (HK) and Co-Founder of the International Proverse Prizes for unpublished writing. He travels frequently to judge public-speaking competitions and regularly adjudicates verse and prose speaking and reading, as well as drama and choral speaking.

Dr Bickley's series of graded poetry anthologies – **POEMS TO ENJOY** – is a well-established tool for learning and teaching English at all levels. Useful notes and a teaching guide are included.

Taken as a whole, this five-book series is suitable for all students, teachers and parents. **Book 1** can be used and enjoyed by Primary 1-3 students and **Book 2** by Primary 4-6 students. **Book 3** can be used and enjoyed by Secondary 1-2 students, **Book 4** by Secondary 3-4 students and **Book 5** by secondary 5-6 students. Students, parents and teachers will enjoy and find useful Dr Bickley's selection of poems.

It is strongly recommended that readers also purchase the Third Edition, which is accompanied by a CD containing lively readings of all poems in the book. These recordings assist pronunciation and help those preparing for solo verse speaking and reading, duo and group-work and choral-speaking in Speech Festivals. They also enhance reading experience.

Parents will welcome this book, in all editions, which gives them the opportunity to read aloud with their children.

THIS BOOK IS A PERENNIAL FAVOURITE.

POEMS TO ENJOY

BOOK THREE

AN ANTHOLOGY OF POEMS

FOR INTERMEDIATE STUDENTS AND READERS

WITH TEACHING AND LEARNING NOTES AND GUIDE

CHOSEN AND EDITED BY

DR VERNER BICKLEY,
MBE, PhD (Lond.), MA, BA (Hons), DipEd, LRAM, LGSM, FCIL, FRSA

Proverse Hong Kong

Poems to Enjoy, Book Three.
Chosen and Edited by Verner Bickley.
With teaching and performance notes by Verner Bickley.
Fifth Edition published in Hong Kong by Proverse Hong Kong, February 2019.
Copyright © Verner Bickley, February 2019.
ISBN: 978-988-8491-59-9

Distribution and other enquiries to: Proverse Hong Kong, P.O.Box 259, Tung Chung Post Office, Tung Chung, Lantau, NT, Hong Kong SAR.
E-mail: proverse@netvigator.com   Web site: www.proversepublishing.com

Illustrations copyright © Proverse Hong Kong.
Page design by Proverse Hong Kong. Cover design, Proverse Hong Kong and Artist Hong Kong Company.

The right of Verner Bickley to be identified as the anthologiser and editor of this work has been asserted by him in accordance with the Copyright, Designs and Patents Act 1988.

All rights reserved. No part of this publication may be reproduced, stored in a retrieval system, or transmitted, in any form or by any means, electronic, mechanical, photocopying, recording or otherwise, without the prior written permission of the publisher or publisher and author. The book is sold subject to the condition that it shall not, by way of trade or otherwise, be lent, re-sold, hired out or otherwise circulated without the publisher's prior written consent in any form of binding or cover other than that in which it is published and without a similar condition including this condition being imposed on the subsequent owner or purchaser. Please contact Proverse Hong Kong in writing, to request any and all permissions (including but not restricted to republishing, inclusion in anthologies, translation, reading, performance and use as set pieces in examinations and festivals).

Poems to Enjoy, Book Three was first published in the United Kingdom in 1960, by University of London Press Ltd (GB SBN 340 07583 X) copyright © Verner Bickley 1960, with Teaching Notes in a separate volume. Copyright © Verner Bickley 1960.
Third edition, with accompanying audio of all poems in the complete anthology. Readers: Verner Bickley and Gillian Bickley. Published in pbk and audio in Hong Kong by Proverse Hong Kong, January 2013.
Copyright © Verner Bickley, January 2013. ISBN 978-988-19934-1-0
Most of the poems in both the 1st and 3rd editions of *Poems to Enjoy*, *Book Three*, were included in the 2nd edition of this work, *Poems to Enjoy* Book 3, part of a 3-book series.

Proverse Hong Kong
    British Library Cataloguing in Publication Data (for 3rd edition, with CD)

Poems to enjoy.
  Book 3. -- 3rd ed.
  1. English poetry. 2. Oral interpretation of poetry--
Juvenile literature. 3. English poetry--Study and teaching
(Secondary) 4. English language--Study and teaching--
Foreign speakers.
I. Bickley, Verner Courtenay.
821'.008-dc23

ISBN-13: 9789881993410

Acknowledgements

For permission to use copyright material thanks are due to the following:
Oxford University Press for 'Johnny Head-in-Air' taken from *Struwwelpeter* by Heinreich Hoffmann; Messrs Macmillan & Co. Ltd and Mrs George Bambridge for 'Rikki-Tikki-Tavi' taken from *Jungle Book* and 'I Keep Six Honest Serving Men' from *Just So Stories* both by Rudyard Kipling; Messrs Macmillan & Co. Ltd and the Trustees of Rabindranath Tagore for 'Fairyland' and 'Paper Boats' taken from *The Crescent Moon*; Messrs. Macmillan & Co. Ltd and Mrs James Stephens for 'The Rivals' and 'The Snare' both from *Collected Poems* of James Stephens; The Macmillan Company, N.Y., for 'The Firemen's Ball' by Vachel Lindsay from his *Collected Poems*; Dr E.V. Rieu for 'Anthony Washed His Face Today' from *CuckooCalling*; Mrs I.M. Flower for 'The Monkey Sailors' by Robin Flower; Houghton Mifflin Company for 'The Plaint of the Camel' by C.E. Carryl; Messrs. William Collins Sons & Co. Ltd for 'The Clothes Line' by Charlotte Druitt Cole; The Society of Authors as Literary Trustees of Walter de la Mare and Messrs. Faber and Faber Ltd for 'Echo', 'Silver', 'The Horseman', 'The Ship of Rio', 'The Lost Shoe' and 'Tartary'; Messrs Methuen & Co. Ltd for 'Duck's Ditty' from *The Wind in the Willows* by Kenneth Grahame; Messrs. Frederick Muller Ltd for 'The Dancing Cabman' by J.B. Morton from *The Dancing Cabman and Other Verses*; Messrs. Chatto & Windus Ltd for 'Lone Dog' by I.R. McLeod from *Songs to Save a Soul*; Captain Francis Newbolt, C.M.G. for 'The Toy Band' from *Poems New and Old* and 'The Nightjar' from *A Perpetual Memory* both by Sir Henry Newbolt and published by Messrs. John Murray Ltd; The Cresset Press for 'At Night' by Francis Cornford and 'The Viper' by Ruth Pitter; Messrs. William Heinemann Ltd; for 'The Palanquin Bearers' taken from *The Golden Threshold* by Sarojini Naidu; Messrs. Routledge & Kegan Paul Ltd for 'Above the Dock' by T.E. Hulme taken from *Speculations*; Messrs Constable & Co. Ltd for 'Pedlar of Spells ' and 'Last Poem' from

Poems to Enjoy, Book Three (5th edition)

170 Chinese Poems by Arthur Waley; The Bodley Head for 'The Hawk' by A. C. Benson taken from *Selected Poems*; Messrs George Allen & Unwin for 'The Kra' taken from *Elements of Folk Psychology* by Wundt translated by Schaub, and 'Flood' by Tao Chien taken from *Chinese Poems* translated by Arthur Waley; Miss Eleanor Farjeon for 'Cats'; Messrs. J.M. Dent & Sons Ltd for 'The Ship' by Richard Church taken from *The Glance Backward;* Hon. Lady Salmond for 'To a Black Greyhound' by Julian Henry Grenfell; Messrs. Samuel French Ltd and Mrs Daisy Drinkwater for 'The Snail' by John Drinkwater; Mrs Barbara Baker for 'A Spike of Green'; The Society of Authors and Dr John Masefield O.M. for 'An Old Song Re-Sung'; Sir John Squire for 'The Ship'; Messrs. Evans Bros. Ltd for 'The Aeroplane' by Jeannie Kirby and 'White Horse' by J.F. Pawsey from *Come Follow Me*; Messrs Basil Blackwell for 'The King of China's Daughter' by Edith Sitwell, 'Cobwebs' by E.L.M. King and 'Wander-Thirst' by Gerald Gould; The Clarendon Press for 'The Cliff Top' from *Shorter Poems of Robert Bridges*; The Society of Authors and Mrs Cicely Binyon for 'The Little Dancers' by Lawrence Binyon; Messrs. John Murray Ltd for 'In Yung-Yang' by Po Chu-i from *A Feast of Lanterns* in the series *Wisdom of the East*; Messrs. William Blackwood and the author for 'Song from the Flower of Old Japan' from *Collected Poems of Alfred Noyes*; Miss Ruth Hendry for 'The Silver Road' and 'The Upside-Down World' both by Hamish Hendry; Lady Cynthia Asquith for 'the Lion' by Herbert Asquith; Miss Mary Daunt for 'The Emperor of China'; Mr Thomas Mark for 'Up and Away'; Mr Edmund Blunden for 'Down Our Street'; and Messrs Gerald Duckworth & Co. Ltd for 'Milk for the Cat: by Harold Munro from *Collected Poems*.

In certain cases it has not been possible to trace the copyright holders. Full acknowledgement of any rights not mentioned here will be made in subsequent editions if notification is received.

Poems to Enjoy, Book Three (5th edition)

To All Students

The poetry in this book has been chosen for you to read and enjoy.

Part One contains poems which you should find interesting to speak, either by yourselves, or in groups arranged in different ways.

Part Two has been called "Pictures in Poetry", because the poems in it describe scenes, persons and animals which, in some instances, will be familiar to you. After you have listened to a poem from this Part you might, perhaps, like to sketch or paint the pictures which you "see" in your mind.

All the poems in **Part Three** tell a story and you should have little difficulty in understanding any of them. Some of the words, of course, will be new to you. But, with help, their meaning will soon become clear.

Compared with all the poems in the world, there are only comparatively few poems in this book. I hope you will enjoy them so much that you will look for others yourself to make your own collection of favourite poems.

After reading and re-reading some of these poems and studying the way in which the poets have set to work, perhaps you will write some of your own?

To All Parents

It is pleasant to share interests and time with children. Poetry is often regarded as difficult. Some is difficult and some is not difficult. The poems in this series are carefully graded, with adequate notes to make reading pleasant and understanding accesible at levels suitable for each reader. Whether or not parents are already in the habit of reading poetry in English, they can enjoy reading the poems in this series of five books, with their children of all ages.

Poems to Enjoy, Book Three (5th edition)

To All Teachers

This book contains a variety of poems of different degrees of difficulty to suit different ways of learning. The poems in Part One are suitable for reading aloud; those in Part Two are largely descriptive; and each poem in Part Three tells a story. The sequence in which the poems are used is, however, at the teacher's discretion.

The poems can be used as supplementary reading material, for oral work, including practice of stress and rhythm, and for different kinds of listening activities. The descriptive poems should develop and challenge the students' imagination and the 'story' or 'narrative' poems are included because all students like to hear or read a good story, provided that they can understand it. In addition to being enjoyed for themselves, the narrative poems provide material for choral work, for dramatization, discussions and questioning.

All the poems in this collection are suitable for extra-curricular work, for example, verse-speaking, choral-speaking, drama, and words and movement.

Poetry can be integrated successfully with the presentation and practice or activities stage of an English lesson, and if emphasis is placed on enjoyment and the students are encouraged to participate fully in the lesson, it can make learning more effective. Poetry develops and broadens the imagination through role-playing, provides training in visual perception, helps in the formation of ideas, and adds a new dimension to group work.

Poetry is an exploration of the possibilities of language which can help the student to construct a new and different framework from that of his own language, acquire different sequences and make forward guesses.

Poems to Enjoy, Book Three (5th edition)

Poems to Speak

This section contains poems which have a pronounced rhythmic and musical quality and which are suitable for reading aloud, whether individually, or in chorus, or groups. Because it requires good breath-control, clear enunciation of consonants and precise shaping of vowels, choral speech is valuable as a way of training both ear and voice for all types of solo-speech. Whether a poem should be spoken by the class as a whole, by soloists, or by different groups of various sizes, depends upon the teacher's own preferences, and, even better, upon the ideas of the students themselves. When groups are required, it is a good idea to keep them constant for choral work in different lessons. In this way, it is possible to distribute the ablest speakers in the class among the various groups.

Some suggestions for choral arrangements are given in the Teaching/Learning Guide at the end of the book. Each poem which is at all suitable for choral work is, of course, open to much variation and the suggestions in the Guide should not therefore be taken as obligatory.

Pictures in Poetry

The poems in this section are intended to enhance the students' ability to visualise, in one form or another, what has been described. If the classroom environment is suitable, two or three poems can sometimes be read to create the right atmosphere for a lesson in which the aim is to encourage the students to sketch from the imagination. Once this atmosphere is achieved, the work can begin. When it is complete, the final results can be collected from individuals and shown to the rest of the group or class. Eventually, the students can be encouraged to make their own anthologies by writing out some of the poems from this collection and illustrating them from their own creative work. Pictures and photographs that are similar to scenes in the poems can be brought to the class to be used as the basis for discussion.

A Tale is Told
The poems in this section can be used as material upon which the students can comment and which they can use as the basis for writing their own stories in prose or verse on related themes. The success of the poetry-writing lesson will depend primarily upon the classroom atmosphere; and interruptions from outside the room should, therefore, be avoided as much as is possible. In the concluding stages of each lesson, the students can read their own poems aloud and be invited to make suggestions and comments.

The Teaching and Learning Notes and Guide
The Teaching and Learning Notes and Guide contain suggestions for choral arrangements; definitions and explanations of words and phrases; suggestions for illustration work and story-writing and questions for discussion.

Timeless and traditional
The books contain traditional and timeless poems, as well as poems that inform us how children and adults thought at different periods of time, including at an earlier period of technological sophistication. The poems express many emotions – tenderness, amusement, wonder – and elicit many others – sympathy, concern, helpfulness. Some are cautionary tales ("The Spider and the Fly", "The Story of Johnny Head-In-Air"). Some encourage cheerfulness ("The Cobblers' Song"), a sense of responsibility ("The Firemen's Ball"), cleanliness ("Anthony Washed His Face Today"). Some of the descriptive poems express and teach observation and appreciation of the natural world. One poem demonstrates how the power of imagination can triumph over circumstances and bring contentment ("Down Our Street").

Poems to Enjoy, Book Three (5th edition)

The audio recording (3rd edition only)
The audio recording gives examples of how two adult English native-speakers who enjoy reading aloud would read the poems. On another occasion, of course, they each might read the poems differently. There is no need to copy or ask students to copy their readings. However, these recordings will be useful in several ways. They will serve to make the meaning of the poems clearer. They offer interpretations of the poems and examples of the use of stress, pause, variety of pitch, enjambement and similar. They give good guidance as to the pronunciation of words that might be less familiar. They are enjoyable in themselves.

Variety may usefully be introduced in the use of the text and the recording. Sometimes, the text could be read first, sometimes the recording could be listened to first. Sometimes both could be used at the same time.

Write to us!
Teachers, students and parents are encouraged to write to us to share their experiences. We would be very interested to know which way of using this book and the related audio recordings was most useful to you. Please also let us know which particular poems your comments relate to. We look forward to hearing from you!

Poems to Enjoy, Book Three (5th edition)

Contents

Acknowledgements   5
To All Students, Parents and Teachers   7

PART ONE: POEMS TO SPEAK

TITLE	AUTHOR	PAGE
The Spider and the Fly	Mary Howitt	18
Rikki-Tikki-Tavi	Rudyard Kipling	21
The Story of Johnny Head-in-Air	Heinrich Hoffman	22
Will you Walk a Little Faster?	Lewis Carroll	24
The Cobblers' Song	John Tilney	26
From The Fireman's Ball	Vachel Lindsay	27
Song of the Graces	George Darley	29
Anthony Washed his Face Today	E. V. Rieu	31
Bee-Song	Anon.	32
When Cats Run Home	Alfred, Lord Tennyson	32
While going the Road	Anon.	33
The Monkey Sailors	Robin Flower	36
The Clothes-Line	Charlotte Druitt Cole	37
The Plaint of the Camel	Charles Edward Carryl	38
Ducks' Ditty	Kenneth Grahame	40
The Twelve Days of Christmas	Old Rhyme	41
The Deaf Woman	Traditional	42
Echo	Walter de la Mare	43
Turtle Soup	Lewis Carroll	44
The Dancing Cabman	J.B. Morton	45
Early in the Morning	Old Sea Shanty	46
Lone Dog	Irene R. McLeod	47

13

Poems to Enjoy, Book Three (5th edition)

PART ONE: POEMS TO SPEAK (contd)

The Drop of Water	Olive March	47
Sir Eglamore	Anon.	49
The Marriage of the Frog and the Mouse	T. Ravenscroft	50
At Night	Frances Cornford	52
Sampan	Tao Lang Pee	53
The Toy Band: A Tale of the Great Retreat	Sir Henry Newbolt	54
The Splendour Falls on Castle Walls	Lord Tennyson	56
A Farmer he Lived in the West Country	Anon.	57

PART TWO: PICTURES IN POETRY

TITLE	AUTHOR	PAGE
Fairyland	Rabindranath Tagore	60
The Palanquin Bearers	Sarojini Naidu	61
The Dismantled Ship	Walt Whitman	62
Silver	Walter de la Mare	62
Above the Dock	T.E. Hulme	63
The Pedlar of Spells	Arthur Waley	63
The Horseman	Walter de la Mare	63
The Hawk	A.C. Benson	64
The Eagle	Lord Tennyson	65
Snail	John Drinkwater	65
The Viper	Ruth Pitter	66
The Ship	Richard Church	67
The Waterhen	Dante Gabriel Rossetti	67
To a Black Greyhound	Julian Grenfell	68
Cats	Eleanor Farjeon	69
From Paper Boats	Rabindranath Tagore	70

Poems to Enjoy, Book Three (5th edition)

PART TWO: PICTURES IN POETRY (contd)

Flood	T'ao Ch'ien (Translated by Arthur Waley)	70
An Old Song Re-Sung	John Masefield	71
The Kra	Anon.	72
The Gallant Ship	Sir Walter Scott	72
A Spike of Green	Barbara Baker	73
The Ship	Sir John Squire	74
The Aeroplane	Jeannie Kirby	75
Cobwebs	E.L.M. King	76
The Rivals	James Stephens	77
The Train	Mary E. Coleridge	78
White Horses	Irene F. Pawsey	79
The Caterpillar	Christina Rossetti	80
The Cliff-Top	Robert Bridges	80
The Little Dancers	Laurence Binyon	81

PART THREE: A TALE IS TOLD

TITLE	AUTHOR	PAGE
The King of China's Daughter	Edith Sitwell	84
In Yung-Yang	Po Chi-i	85
The Ship of Rio	Walter de la Mare	86
Last Poem	Po Chu-i	87
The Snare	James Stephens	88
The Lost Shoe	Walter de la Mare	89
Oh! Cruel Were My Parients	Anon.	91
I Keep Six Honest Serving-Men	Rudyard Kipling	92
The Seven Fiddlers	Sebastian Evans	93
Soldier, Won't you Marry Me?	Anon.	95
The Fisher's Widow	Arthur Symons	97

Poems to Enjoy, Book Three (5th edition)

PART THREE: A TALE IS TOLD (contd)

Song from The Flower of Old Japan	Alfred Noyes	98
The Nightjar	Sir Henry Newbolt	99
The Upside-Down World	Hamish Hendry	100
The Hag	Robert Herrick	101
The Silver Road	Hamish Hendry	102
The Ballad of Earl Haldan's Daughter	Charles Kingsley	103
Tartary	Walter de la Mare	104
Eldorado	Edgar Allan Poe	106
The Lion	Herbert Asquith	107
Hiawatha's Childhood	H.W. Longfellow	108
Wander-Thirst	Gerald Gould	110
The Minstrel Boy	Thomas Moore	111
The Emperor of China	Mary Daunt	112
Down our Street	Edmund Blunden	114
Milk for the Cat	Harold Monro	115
Up and Away	T. Mark	117
Two Red Roses Across the Moon	William Morris	119
Boot and Saddle	Robert Browning	121

Teaching and Learning Notes and Guide	123
About the Editor	149
About Proverse Hong Kong / The Proverse Prizes	151

Part One

Poems to Speak

Poems to Enjoy, Book Three (5th edition)

THE SPIDER AND THE FLY

Spider: Will you walk into my parlour?
Chorus: Said the spider to the fly.
Spider: 'Tis the prettiest little parlour
That you ever did espy.
The way into my parlour
Is up a winding stair;
And I have many curious things
To show you when you're there.

Fly: Oh, no, no.
Chorus: Said the little fly.
Fly: To ask me is in vain;
For who goes up your winding stair
Can ne'er come down again.

Spider: I'm sure you must be very weary, dear,
With soaring up so high;
Will you rest upon my little bed?
Chorus: Said the spider to the fly.
Spider: There are pretty curtains drawn around;
The sheets are fine and thin,
And if you like to rest awhile
I'll snugly tuck you in.

Fly: Oh, no, no.
Chorus: Said the little fly.
Fly: For I've often heard it said,
They never, never wake again
Who sleep upon your bed!

Chorus: Said the cunning spider to the fly.
Spider: Dear friend, what can I do
To prove the warm affection
I've always felt for you?

Fly: I thank you, gentle sir,
For what you're pleased to say,
And bidding you good morning, now,
I'll call another day.

Chorus: The spider turned him round about,
And went into his den,
For well he knew the silly fly
Would soon come back again;
So he wove a subtle web
In a little corner sly,
And set his table ready
To dine upon the fly.
Then he came out to his door again
And merrily did sing—

Spider: Come hither, hither, pretty fly,
With the pearl and silver wing;
Your robes are green and purple.
There's a crest upon your head.
Your eyes are like the diamond bright,
But mine are dull as lead!

Chorus: Alas! alas! How very soon
This silly little fly,
Hearing his wily, flattering words
Came slowly flitting by.
With buzzing wings she hung aloft
Then near and nearer drew,
Thinking only of her brilliant eyes,

Her green and purple hue.
Thinking only of her crested head—
Poor, foolish thing! At last
Up jumped the cunning spider
And fiercely held her fast.
He dragged her up his winding stair,
Into his dismal den,
Within his little parlour,
And she ne'er came out again.

And now, dear little children,
Who may this story read,
To idle, flattering words
I pray you, ne'er give heed;
Unto an evil counsellor
Close heart and ear and eye,
And take a lesson from this tale
Of the spider and the fly.

Mary Howitt

Poems to Enjoy, Book Three (5th edition)

RIKKI TIKKI TAVI
(A fight between a mongoose and a cobra)

At the hole where he went in
Red-Eye called to Wrinkle-Skin.
Hear what little Red-Eye saith:
"Nag, come up and dance with death!"

Eye to eye and head to head,
    (Keep the measure, Nag.)
This shall end when one is dead;
    (At thy pleasure, Nag.)

Turn for turn and twist for twist—
    (Run and hide thee, Nag)
Hah! The hooded Death has missed!
    (Woe betide thee, Nag!)

Rudyard Kipling

Poems to Enjoy, Book Three (5th edition)

THE STORY OF JOHNNY HEAD-IN-AIR

As he trudged along to school,
It was always Johnny's rule
To be looking at the sky
And the clouds that floated by:
But what just before him lay,
In his way,
Johnny never thought about;
So that everyone cried out:
"Look at little Johnny there,
Little Johnny Head-In-Air!"

Running just in Johnny's way,
Came a little dog one day;
Johnny's eyes were still astray
Up on high,
In the sky,
And he never heard them cry:
"Johnny, mind, the dog is nigh!"
Bump!
Bump!
Down they fell with such a thump,
Dog and Johnny in a lump!

Once, with head as high as ever,
Johnny walked beside the river.
Johnny watched the swallows trying
Which was cleverest at flying.
Oh! What fun!
Johnny watched the bright round sun
Going in and coming out;
This was all he thought about.

So he strode on, only think!
To the river's very brink,
Where the bank was high and steep,
And the water very deep;
And the fishes, in a row,
Stared to see him coming so.

One step more! Oh! sad to tell!
Headlong in poor Johnny fell,
And the fishes, in dismay,
Wagged their tails and swam away.
There lay Johnny on his face,
With his nice red writing-case;
But, as they were passing by,
Two strong men had heard him cry;
And, with sticks, these two strong men
Hooked poor Johnny out again.

Oh! you should have seen him shiver
When they pulled him from the river.
He was in a sorry plight!
Dripping wet, and such a fright!

Poems to Enjoy, Book Three (5th edition)

Wet all over, everywhere,
Clothes, and arms, and face, and hair:
Johnny never will forget
What it is to be so wet.

And the fishes, one, two, three,
Are come back again, you see;
Up they came the moment after,
To enjoy the fun and laughter.
Each popped out his little head,
And to tease poor Johnny, said:
"Silly little Johnny, look,
You have lost your writing-book!"

Heinrich Hoffmann

WILL YOU WALK A LITTLE FASTER?

"Will you walk a little faster?" said a whiting to a snail.
"There's a porpoise close behind us, and he's treading on my
 tail.
See how eagerly the lobsters and the turtles all advance!
They are waiting on the shingle—will you come and join the
 dance?
Will you, won't you, will you, won't you, will you join the
 dance?
Will you, won't you, will you, won't you, won't you join the
 dance?

"You can really have no notion how delightful it will be,
When they take us up and throw us, with the lobsters, out to
 sea!"
But the snail replied "Too far, too far!" and gave a look
 askance—

Said he thanked the whiting kindly, but he would not join the
  dance.
Would not, could not, would not, could not, could not join the
  dance.
Would not, could not, would not, could not, could not join the
  dance.

"What matters it how far we go?" his scaly friend replied.
"There is another shore, you know, upon the other side.
The further off from England the nearer is to France—
Then turn not pale, beloved snail, but come and join the dance.
Will you, won't you, will you, won't you, will you join the
  dance?
Will you, won't you, will you, won't you, won't you join the
  dance?"

Lewis Carroll

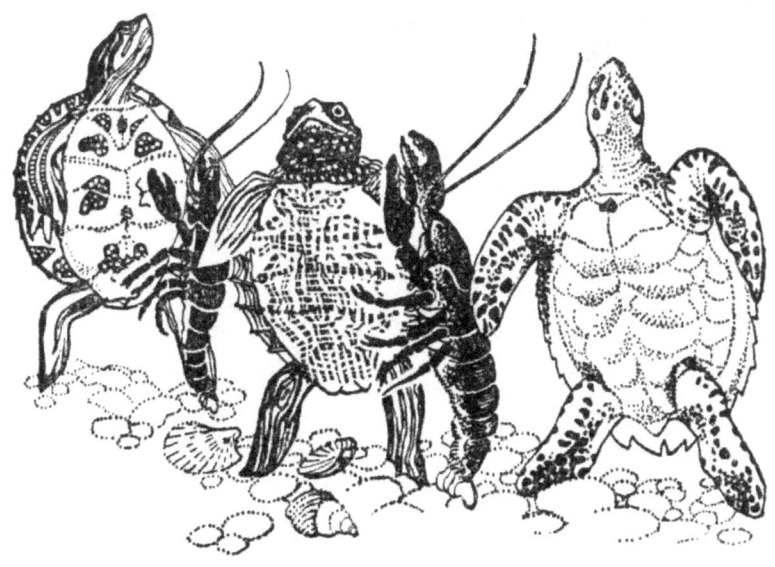

Poems to Enjoy, Book Three (5th edition)

THE COBBLERS' SONG

Cobblers	We cobblers lead a merry life.
Chorus	Dan, dan, dan, dan.
Cobblers	Void of all envy and of strife,
Chorus	Dan, diddle, dan.
Cobblers	Our ease is great, our labour small,
Chorus	Dan, dan, dan, dan.
Cobblers	And yet our gains be much withal,
Chorus	Dan, diddle, dan.
Cobblers	With this art so fine and fair,
Chorus	Dan, dan, dan, dan.
Cobblers	No occupation may compare,
Chorus	Dan, diddle, dan.
Cobblers	For merry pastime and joyful glee,
Chorus	Dan, dan, dan, dan.
Cobblers	Most happy men we cobblers be,
Chorus	Dan, diddle, dan.
Cobblers	This brings us to a merry mood,
Chorus	Dan, diddle, dan.

John Tilney

From THE FIREMEN'S BALL

"Give the engines room,
Give the engines room."
Louder, faster,
The little band-master
Whips up the fluting,
Hurries up the tooting.
He thinks that he stands,
The reins in his hands,
In the fire-chief's place
In the night alarm chase.
The cymbals whang,
The kettledrums bang—
"Clear the street,
Clear the street,
Clear the street—Boom, boom.
In the evening gloom,
In the evening gloom,
Give the engines room,
Lest souls be trapped
In a terrible tomb."
The sparks and the pine-brands
Whirl on high
From the black and reeking alleys
To the wide red sky.
Hear the hot glass crashing,
Of the firemen's ball.
Listen to the music
Of the firemen's ball.

Poems to Enjoy, Book Three (5th edition)

"'Tis the
NIGHT
Of doom,"
Say the ding-dong doom bells.
"NIGHT
Of doom,"
Say the ding-dong doom bells.
Whangaranga, whangaranga,
Whang, whang, whang,
Clang, clang, clangaranga,
Clang, clang, clang.
Clang—a—ranga,
Clang—a—ranga,
Clang—a—ranga
Clang—
Clang—
Clang—
Listen—to—the—music—
Of the firemen's ball—

Vachel Lindsay

SONG OF THE GRACES

We the Sun's bright daughters be!
   As our golden wings may show;
Every land and every sea
   Echoes our sweet ho-ran ho!

    Round, and round, and round we go
    Singing our sweet ho-ran ho!

Over heath and over hill,
   Ho-ran, hi-ran, ho-ran ho!
At the wind's unruly will,

    Round, and round, and round we go
    Singing our sweet ho-ran ho!

Through the desert valley green,
   Ho-ran, hi-ran, ho-ran ho!
Lonely mountain cliffs between,

    Round, and round, and round we go
    Singing our sweet ho-ran ho!

Into cave and into wood,
   Ho-ran, hi-ran, ho-ran ho!
Light as bubbles down the flood,

    Round, and round, and round we go
    Singing our sweet ho-ran ho!

By the many tassell'd bower,
   Ho-ran, hi-ran, ho-ran ho!
Nimming precious bosom-flower,

Poems to Enjoy, Book Three (5th edition)

    Round, and round, and round we go
    Singing our sweet ho-ran ho!

After bee, and after gnat,
    Ho-ran, hi-ran, ho-ran ho!
Hunting bird and chasing bat,

    Round, and round, and round we go
    Singing our sweet ho-ran ho!

To the East and to the West,
    Ho-ran, hi-ran, ho-ran ho!
To the place that we love best.

    Round, and round, and round we go
    Singing our sweet ho-ran ho!

George Darley

Poems to Enjoy, Book Three (5th edition)

ANTHONY WASHED HIS FACE TODAY

Anthony washed his face today—
    Nobody made him do it:
He wasn't told in the usual way;
    Nobody helped him through it.

He smiled his usual smile before,
    And teased his little sister;
Rose, but stopped on his way to the door;
    Thought a moment, and kissed her;

Turned and went of his own accord,
    With a stern but high demeanour;
And came back looking a trifle bored—
    But more than a trifle cleaner.

Anthony, Anthony, are you ill?
    Or is my eyesight failing?
You've washed your face of your own free will—
    Anthony, are you ailing?

E.V. Rieu

Poems to Enjoy, Book Three (5th edition)

BEE-SONG

Buzz, buzz, buzz!
Ring out your kettle
Of purest mettle
To settle, to settle,
Your swarm of bees!
For men new wiving
The way to be thriving
Is hiving, hiving;
Then no time leese
To hive your bees.

Anon.

WHEN CATS RUN HOME

When cats run home and light is come,
And dew is cold upon the ground,
And the far-off stream is dumb,
And the whirring sail goes round:
And the whirring sail goes round:
Alone and warming his five wits,
The white owl in the belfry sits.

Alfred, Lord Tennyson

WHILE GOING THE ROAD

While going the road to sweet Athy,
  Hurroo! Hurroo!
While going the road to sweet Athy,
  Hurroo! Hurroo!
While going the road to sweet Athy,
A stick in my hand and a drop in my eye,
A doleful damsel I heard cry:
  "Och, Johnny, I hardly knew ye!
With drums and guns, and guns and drums
  The enemy nearly slew ye,
  My darling dear, you look so queer,
  Och, Johnny, I hardly knew ye!

"Where are your eyes that looked so mild?
  Hurroo! Hurroo!
Where are your eyes that looked so mild?
  Hurroo! Hurroo!
Where are your eyes that looked so mild?
When my poor heart you first beguiled?
Why did you run from me and the child?
  Och, Johnny, I hardly knew ye!
With drums, *etc.*

"Where are the legs with which you run?
  Hurroo! Hurroo!
Where are the legs with which you run?
  Hurroo! Hurroo!
Where are the legs with which you run
When you went to carry a gun?—
Indeed your dancing days are done!
  Och, Johnny, I hardly knew ye!
With drums, *etc.*

Poems to Enjoy, Book Three (5th edition)

"It grieved my heart to see you sail,
   Hurroo! Hurroo!
It grieved my heart to see you sail,
   Hurroo! Hurroo!
It grieved my heart to see you sail
Though from my heart you took leg bail—
Like a cod you're doubled up head and tail.
   Och, Johnny, I hardly knew ye!
With drums, *etc.*

"You haven't an arm and you haven't a leg,
   Hurroo! Hurroo!
You haven't an arm and you haven't a leg,
   Hurroo! Hurroo!
You haven't an arm and you haven't a leg,
You're an eyeless, noseless, chickenless egg;
You'll have to be put in a bowl to beg;
   Och, Johnny, I hardly knew ye!
With drums, *etc.*

"I'm happy for to see you home,
   Hurroo! Hurroo!
I'm happy for to see you home,
   Hurroo! Hurroo!
I'm happy for to see you home,
All from the island of Sulloon,
So low in flesh, so high in bone,
   Och, Johnny, I hardly knew ye!
With drums, *etc.*

"But sad as it is to see you so,
   Hurroo! Hurroo!
But sad as it is to see you so,
   Hurroo! Hurroo!
But sad as it is to see you so,

And to think of you now as an object of woe,
Your Peggy'll still keep ye on as her beau;
   Och, Johnny, I hardly knew ye!
With drums and guns and guns and drums
   The enemy nearly slew ye,
   My darling dear, you look so queer,
   Och, Johnny, I hardly knew ye!"

Anon.

Poems to Enjoy, Book Three (5th edition)

THE MONKEY SAILORS

The parrots squall
And the buffaloes bawl
And we, we all,
Sing and go,
Tail and toe,
Diddle-de-dee,
From tree to tree;
Scuttle in glee,
One after another,
Brother and brother,
Dancing, swinging,
Falling, clinging,
You by the hand,
I by the tail,
Like boats on land
We sail and sail,
And the leaves are waves on a green, green sea,
But there never was a sailor so happy as we.

Robin Flower

Poems to Enjoy, Book Three (5th edition)

THE CLOTHES-LINE

Hand in hand they dance in a row,
Hither and thither, and to and fro,
Flip! Flap! Flop! and away they go—
Fluttering creatures as white as snow.
Like restive horses they caper and prance;
Like fairy-tale witches they wildly dance;
Rounded in front, but hollow behind,
They shiver and skip in the merry March wind.
One I saw dancing excitedly,
Struggling so wildly till she was free,
Then, leaving pegs and clothes-line behind her,
She flew like a bird, and no one could find her.
I saw her gleam like a sail, in the sun,
Flipping and flapping, and flopping for fun.
Nobody knows where she now can be,
Hid in a ditch, or drowned in the sea.
She was my handkerchief not long ago,
But she'll never come back to my pocket, I know.

Charlotte Druitt Cole

Poems to Enjoy, Book Three (5th edition)

THE PLAINT OF THE CAMEL

Canary-birds feed on sugar and seed,
Parrots have crackers to crunch;
And as for the poodles, they tell me the noodles
Have chicken and cream for their lunch.
   But there's never a question
   About my digestion,
   ANYTHING does for me.

Cats, you're aware, can repose in a chair,
Chickens can roost upon rails;
Puppies are able to sleep in a stable,
And oysters can slumber in pails.
   But no one supposes
   A poor Camel reposes.
   ANY PLACE does for me.

Lambs are enclosed where it's never exposed,
Coops are constructed for hens;
Kittens are treated to houses well heated,
And pigs are protected by pens.
   But a Camel comes handy
   Wherever it's sandy,
   ANYWHERE does for me.

People would laugh if you rode a giraffe,
Or mounted the back of an ox;
It's nobody's habit to ride on a rabbit,
Or try to bestraddle a fox.
   But as for a Camel, he's
   Ridden by families—
   ANY LOAD does for me.

Poems to Enjoy, Book Three (5th edition)

A snake is as round as a hole in the ground;
Weasels are wavy and sleek;
And no alligator could ever be straighter
Than lizards that live in a creek.
   But a Camel's all lumpy,
   And bumpy, and humpy,
   ANY SHAPE does for me.

Charles Edward Carryl

Poems to Enjoy, Book Three (5th edition)

DUCKS' DITTY

All along the backwater,
Through the rushes tall,
Ducks are a-dabbling,
   Up tails all!

Ducks' tails, drakes' tails,
Yellow feet a-quiver,
Yellow bills all out of sight
   Busy in the river!

Slushy green undergrowth
Where the roach swim—
Here we keep our larder
   Cool and full and dim!

Every one for what he likes!
We like to be
Heads down, tails up,
   Dabbling free!

High in the blue above
Swifts whirl and call—
We are down a-dabbling
   Up tails all!

Kenneth Grahame

Poems to Enjoy, Book Three (5th edition)

THE TWELVE DAYS OF CHRISTMAS

On the twelve Days of Christmas,
My true love sent to me:
Twelve drummers drumming,
Eleven pipers piping,
Ten lords a-leaping,
Nine ladies dancing,
Eight maids a-milking,
Seven swans a-swimming,
Six ducks a-laying,
Five gold rings,
Four French hens,
Three calling birds,
Two turtle doves
And a partridge in a pear tree.

Old Rhyme

Poems to Enjoy, Book Three (5th edition)

THE DEAF WOMAN

"Old woman, old woman, are you fond of smoking?
Old woman, old woman, are you fond of smoking?"
"Speak a little louder, sir, I'm rather hard of hearing.
Speak a little louder, sir, I'm rather hard of hearing."

"Old woman, old woman, are you fond of carding?"
Old woman, old woman, are you fond of carding?"
"Speak a little louder, sir, I'm rather hard of hearing.
Speak a little louder, sir, I'm rather hard of hearing."

"Old woman, old woman, will you let me court you?
Old woman, old woman, will you let me court you?"
"Speak a little louder, sir, I just begin to hear you.
Speak a little louder, sir, I just begin to hear you."

"Old woman, old woman, don't you want to marry me?
Old woman, old woman, don't you want to marry me?"
"Lord have mercy on my soul! I think that now I hear you.
Lord have mercy on my soul! I think that now I hear you."

Traditional

ECHO

"Who called?" I said, and the words
    Through the whispering glades,
Hither, thither, baffled the birds—
    "Who called? Who called?"

The leafy boughs on high,
    Hissed in the sun;
The dark air carried my cry
    Faintingly on:

Eyes in the green, in the shade,
    In the motionless brake,
Voices that said what I said,
    For mockery's sake:

"Who cares?" I bawled through my tears;
    The wind fell low:
In the silence, "Who cares? Who cares?"
    Wailed to and fro.

Walter de la Mare

Poems to Enjoy, Book Three (5th edition)

TURTLE SOUP

Beautiful soup, so rich and green,
Waiting in a hot tureen!
Who for such dainties would not stoop?
Soup of the evening, beautiful soup!
Soup of the evening, beautiful soup!
Beau—ootiful—soo—oop!
Beau—ootiful—soo—oop!
Soo—oop—of the e—e—evening
Beautiful, beautiful soup!

Beautiful soup! Who cares for fish,
Game, or any other dish?
Who would not give all else for two
Pennyworth only of beautiful soup?
Pennyworth only of beautiful soup?
Beau—ootiful—soo—oop!
Beau—ootiful—soo—opp!
Soo—oop of the e—e—evening,
Beautiful, beauti—FUL SOUP!

Lewis Carroll

THE DANCING CABMAN

Alone on the lawn
   The cabman dances;
In the dew of the dawn
   He kicks and prances.
His bowler is set
   On his bullet head,
For his boots are wet
   And his aunt is dead.

There on the lawn
   As the light advances,
On the tide of the dawn
   The cabman dances.
Swift and strong
   As a garden roller,
He dances along
   In his little bowler,
Skimming the lawn
   With royal grace
The dew of the dawn
   On his great red face.

To fairy flutes,
   As the light advances,
In square black boots
   The cabman dances.

J.B. Morton

Poems to Enjoy, Book Three (5th edition)

EARLY IN THE MORNING

What shall we do with the drunken sailor,
What shall we do with the drunken sailor,
What shall we do with the drunken sailor,
   Early in the morning?
      Hooray and up she rises,
      Hooray and up she rises,
      Hooray and up she rises
         Early in the morning.

Put him in the long boat until he's sober, *etc.*
    Hooray and up she rises, *etc.*

Pull out the plug and wet him all over, *etc.*
    Hooray and up she rises, *etc.*

Put him in the scuppers with a hose-pipe on him, *etc.*
    Hooray and up she rises, *etc.*

Heave him by the leg in a running bowline, *etc.*
    Hooray and up she rises, *etc.*

Tie him to the taffrail when she's yard-arm under, *etc.*
    Hooray and up she rises, *etc.*

Old Sea Shanty

Poems to Enjoy, Book Three (5th edition)

LONE DOG

I'm a lean dog, a keen dog, a wild dog, and lone;
I'm a rough dog, a tough dog, hunting on my own;
I'm a bad dog, a mad dog, teasing silly sheep;
I love to sit and bay the moon, to keep fat souls from sleep.

I'll never be a lap dog, licking dirty feet,
A sleek dog, a meek dog, cringing for my meat,
Not for me the fireside, the well-filled plate,
But shut door, and sharp stone, and cuff, and kick, and hate.

Not for me the other dogs, running by my side,
Some have run a short while, but none of them would bide,
O mine is still the lone trail, the hard trail, the best,
Wild wind, and wild stars, and the hunger of the quest!

Irene R. McLeod

THE DROP OF WATER

Over the stone fell a drip,
A shimmering, shining slip
Of water—drip, drop, drip!

Drop!
Drip!
Never
Stop!
Drip!
Drop!

Poems to Enjoy, Book Three (5th edition)

Yesterday
From far away
A Will-o'-the-Wisp
Came this way,
Laid her lip
To mine to sip,
Drop!
Drip!

A warm, white lip!
She ran to the top,
To the tip
Of the larch there,
And her hair
Flew in the air.
I called: "Drip! Drop!
Stay, Wisp! Stop!"
Drip!
Drop!

She would not stay—
She did not hear!
She was an evil
Fairy, sure:
I was a drip,
A drop before
She kissed my brow
With her lip, her lip,
And now—
I am a tear.
Drop!
Drip!

Olive March

SIR EGLAMORE

Sir Eglamore, that valiant knight,
    Fa la lanky down dilly,
He took up his sword and he went for to fight,
    Fa la lanky down dilly,
As he rode o'er hill and dale,
All armèd with a coat of mail,
    Fa la lanky down dilly,
There starts a huge dragon out of his den,
    Fa la lanky down dilly,
Which had killed I know not how many men,
    Fa la lanky down dilly.
But when he sees Sir Eglamore,
If you'd but heard how the dragon did roar!
    Fa la lanky down dilly.

This dragon had a plaguey hard hide,
    Fa la lanky down dilly,
Which could the strongest steel abide;
Fa la lanky down dilly,
But as the dragon yawning did fall,
He thrust his sword down, hilt and all,
    Fa la lanky down dilly.
The dragon laid him down and roared,
    Fa la lanky down dilly.
The knight was sorry for his sword;
    Fa la lanky down dilly.
The sword it was a right good blade,
As ever Turk or Spaniard made,
    Fa la lanky down dilly.

Poems to Enjoy, Book Three (5th edition)

When all was done, to the ale-house he went,
    Fa la lanky down dilly,
And presently his twopence was spent,
    Fa la lanky down dilly.
He was so hot with fighting the dragon,
That naught could quench his thirst but a flagon,
    Fa la lanky down dilly.
Well, now let us pray for the King and the Queen,
    Fa la lanky down dilly,
And eke in London town that may be seen,
    Fa la lanky down dilly,
As many knights and as many more
And all as good as Sir Eglamore,
    Fa la lanky down dilly.

Anon.

THE MARRIAGE OF THE FROG AND THE MOUSE

It was the frog in the well,
    Humbledum, humbledum,
And the merry mouse in the mill,
    Tweedle, tweedle, twino.

The frog would a-wooing ride
Sword and buckler by his side.

When he upon his high horse set,
His boots they shone as black as jet.

When he came to the merry mill-pin,
"Lady Mouse, be you within?"

Then came out the dusty mouse:
"I am lady of this house:

"Hast thou any mind of me?"
"I have e'en great mind of thee!"

"Who shall this marriage make?"
"Our Lord which is the rat."

"What shall we have to our supper?"
"Three beans in a pound of butter!"

When supper they were at,
The frog, the mouse and e'en the rat;

Then came in Gib our cat,
And catched the mouse e'en by the back.

Then did they separate,
And the frog leaped on the floor so flat.

Then came in Dick our drake,
And drew the frog e'en to the lake.

The rat ran up the wall,
    Humbledum, humbledum;
A goodly company, the Devil go with all!
    Tweedle, tweedle, twino.

T. Ravenscroft

Poems to Enjoy, Book Three (5th edition)

AT NIGHT

On moony nights the dogs bark shrill
Down the valley and up the hill.

There's one is angry to behold
The moon, so unafraid and cold,
Who makes the earth as bright as day,
But yet unhappy, dead and grey.

Another in his strawy lair
Says, "Who's a-howling over there?
By heavens, I will stop him soon
From interfering with the moon!"

So back he barks, with throat upthrown:
"You leave our moon, our moon alone!"
And other distant dogs respond
Beyond the field, beyond, beyond...

Frances Cornford

SAMPAN

Waves lap lap
Fish fins clap clap
Brown sails flap flap
Chop-sticks tap tap

Up and down the long green river
Ohe Ohe lanterns quiver
Willow branches brush the river
Ohe Ohe lanterns quiver

Waves lap lap
Fish fins clap clap
Brown sails flap flap
Chop-sticks tap tap.

Tao Lang Pee

Poems to Enjoy, Book Three (5th edition)

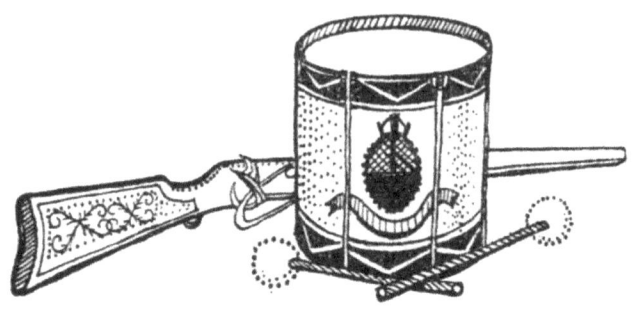

THE TOY BAND: A TALE OF THE GREAT RETREAT

Dreary lay the long road, dreary lay the town,
    Lights out and never a glint o' moon:
Weary lay the stragglers, half a thousand down,
    Sad sighed the weary big Dragoon.
"Oh, if I'd a drum here to make them take the road again,
    Oh! if I'd a fife to wheedle—come boys, come!
You that mean to fight it out, wake and take your load again,
    Fall in! Fall in! Follow the fife and drum!"

"Hey, but here's a toy shop, here's a drum for me,
    Penny whistles too to play the tune!
Half a thousand dead men soon shall hear and see
    We're a band!" said the weary big Dragoon.
"Rubadub! Rubadub! Wake and take the road again,
    Wheedle—deedle—deedle dee, come boys, come!
You that mean to fight it out, wake and take your load again,
    Fall in! Fall in! Follow the fife and drum!"

Poems to Enjoy, Book Three (5th edition)

Cheerly goes the dark road, cheerly goes the night,
   Cheerly goes the blood to keep the beat:
Half a thousand dead men marching on to fight
   With a little penny drum to lift their feet.
"Rubadub! Rubadub! Wake and take the road again,
   Wheedle—deedle—deedle dee, come boys, come!
You that mean to fight it out, wake and take your load again,
   Fall in! Fall in! Follow the fife and drum!"

As long as there's an Englishman to ask a tale of me,
   As long as I can tell the tale aright,
We'll not forget the penny whistle's wheedle—deedle—dee,
   And the big Dragoon a-beating down the night,
"Rubadub! Rubadub! Wake and take the road again,
   Wheedle—deedle—deedle—dee, come boys, come!
You that mean to fight it out, wake and take your load again,
   Fall in! Fall in! Follow the fife and drum!"

Sir Henry Newbolt

Poems to Enjoy, Book Three (5th edition)

THE SPLENDOUR FALLS ON CASTLE WALLS

The splendour falls on castle walls
   And snowy summits old in story:
The long light shakes across the lakes,
   And the wild cataract leaps in glory.
Blow, bugle, blow, set the wild echoes flying,
Blow, bugle; answer, echoes, dying, dying, dying.

O hark, O hear! How thin and clear,
   And thinner, clearer, farther going!
O sweet and far from cliff and scar
   The horns of Elfland faintly blowing!
Blow, let us hear the purple glens replying:
Blow, bugle; answer, echoes, dying, dying, dying.

O love, they die in yon rich sky,
   They faint on hill or field or river:
Our echoes roll from soul to soul,
   And grow for ever and for ever.
Blow, bugle, blow, set the wild echoes flying,
And answer, echoes, answer, dying, dying, dying.

Alfred, Lord Tennyson

A FARMER HE LIVED IN THE WEST COUNTRY

A Farmer he lived in the West Country,
    Bow down! Bow down!
A Farmer he lived in the West Country
And he had daughters one, two and three,
Singing, "I will be true unto my love
If my love will be true unto me."

One day they walked by the river's brim,
    Bow down! Bow down!
One day they walked by the river's brim
When the eldest pushed the youngest in,
Singing, "I will be true unto my love
If my love will be true unto me."

"O sister, O sister, pray lend me your hand,"
    Bow down! Bow down!
"O sister, O sister, pray lend me your hand
And I'll give you both house and land,"
Singing, "I will be true unto my love
If my love will be true unto me."

"I'll neither lend you hand nor glove,"
    Bow down! Bow down!
"I'll neither lend you hand nor glove
Unless you'll promise me your true love,"
Singing, "I will be true unto my love
If my love will be true unto me."

So down the river the maiden swam,
    Bow down! Bow down!
So down the river the maiden swam
Until she came to the miller's dam,
Singing, "I will be true unto my love
If my love will be true unto me."

The miller's daughter stood at the door,
    Bow down! Bow down!
The miller's daughter stood at the door
Blooming like a gilliflower,
Singing, "I will be true unto my love
If my love will be true unto me."

"O father, O father, here swims a swan,"
    Bow down! Bow down!
"O father, O father, here swims a swan
Very much like a gentlewoman,"
Singing, "I will be true unto my love
If my love will be true unto me."

The miller he took his rod and hook,
    Bow down! Bow down!
The miller he took his rod and hook.
And he fished the fair maiden out of the brook,
Singing, "I will be true unto my love
If my love will be true unto me."
    Anon.

Part Two

Pictures in Poetry

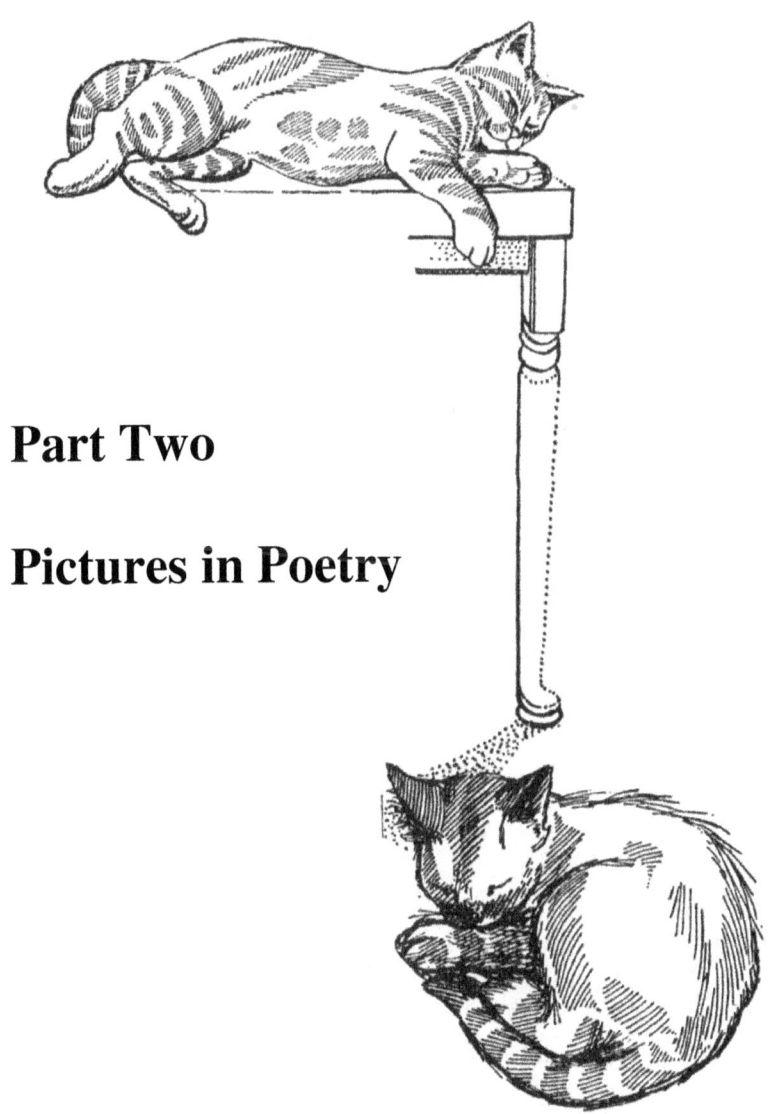

Poems to Enjoy, Book Three (5th edition)

FAIRYLAND

If people came to know where my king's palace is, it would
 vanish into the air.
The walls are of white silver and the roof of shining gold.
The queen lives in a palace with seven courtyards, and she
 wears a jewel that cost all the wealth of seven kingdoms.
But let me tell you, Mother, in a whisper, where my king's
 palace is.
It is at the corner of our terrace where the pot of the *tulsi* plant
 stands.

The princess lies sleeping on the far-away shore of the
 impassable seas.
There is none in the world who can find her but myself.
She has bracelets on her arms and pearl drops in her ears; her
 hair sweeps down upon the floor.
She will wake when I touch her with my magic wand,
 and jewels will fall from her lips when she smiles.
But let me whisper in your ear, Mother; she is

There in the corner of our terrace where the pot of the *tulsi* plant stands.

When it is time for you to go to the river for your bath, step up to that terrace on the roof.
I sit in the corner where the shadows of the walls meet together.
Only puss is allowed to come in with me, for she knows where the barber in the story lives.
But let me whisper, Mother, in your ear where the barber in the story lives.
It is at the corner of the terrace where the pot of the *tulsi* plant stands.

Rabindranath Tagore

THE PALANQUIN BEARERS

Lightly, O lightly we bear her along,
She sways like a flower in the wind of our song;
She skims like a bird on the foam of a stream,
She floats like a laugh from the lips of a dream.
Gaily, O gaily we glide and we sing,
We bear her along like a pearl on a string.
Softly, O softly we bear her along,
She hangs like a star in the dew of our song;
She springs like a beam on the brow of the tide,
She falls like a tear from the eyes of a bride.
Lightly, O lightly we glide and we sing,
We bear her along like a pearl on a string.

Sarojini Naidu

Poems to Enjoy, Book Three (5th edition)

THE DISMANTLED SHIP

In some unused lagoon, some nameless bay,
On sluggish, lonesome waters, anchor'd near the shore,
An old, dismasted, grey and batter'd ship, disabled, done,
After free voyages to all the seas of earth, haul'd up at last, and hawser'd tight,
Lies rusting, mouldering.

Walt Whitman

SILVER

Slowly, silently, now the moon
Walks the night in her silver shoon;
This way, and that, she peers and sees
Silver fruit upon silver trees;
One by one the casements catch
Her beams beneath the silvery thatch;
Couched in his kennel, like a log,
With paws of silver sleeps the dog;
From their shadowy cote the white breasts peep
Of doves in a silver-feathered sleep;
A harvest mouse goes scampering by,
With silver claws, and silver eye;
And moveless fish in the water gleam,
By silver reeds in a silver stream.

Walter de la Mare

ABOVE THE DOCK

Above the quiet dock at midnight,
Tangled in the tall mast's corded height,
Hangs the moon. What seemed so far away
Is but a child's balloon, forgotten after play.

T.E. Hulme

THE PEDLAR OF SPELLS

An old man selling charms in a cranny of the town wall.
He writes out spells to bless the silkworm and spells to protect
    the corn.
With the money he gets each day he only buys wine.
But he does not worry when his legs get wobbly,
For he has a boy to lean on.

Arthur Waley

THE HORSEMAN

I heard a horseman
Ride over the hill;
The moon shone clear,
The night was still;
His helm was silver,
And pale was he;
And the horse he rode
Was of ivory.

Walter de la Mare

Poems to Enjoy, Book Three (5th edition)

THE HAWK

The hawk slipt out of the pine, and rose in the sunlit air:
Steady and still he poised; his shadow slept on the grass:
And the bird's song sickened and sank: she cowered with furtive stare
Dumb, till the quivering dimness should flicker and shift and pass.

Suddenly down he dropped: she heard the hiss of his wing,
Fled with a scream of terror: oh, would she had dared to rest!
For the hawk at eve was full, and there was no bird to sing.
And over the heather drifted the down from a bleeding breast.

A.C. Benson

Poems to Enjoy, Book Three (5th edition)

THE EAGLE

He clasps the crag with crooked hands;
Close to the sun in lonely lands,
Ring'd with the azure world, he stands.

The wrinkled sea beneath him crawls;
He watches from his mountain walls,
And like a thunderbolt he falls.

Alfred Lord Tennyson

SNAIL

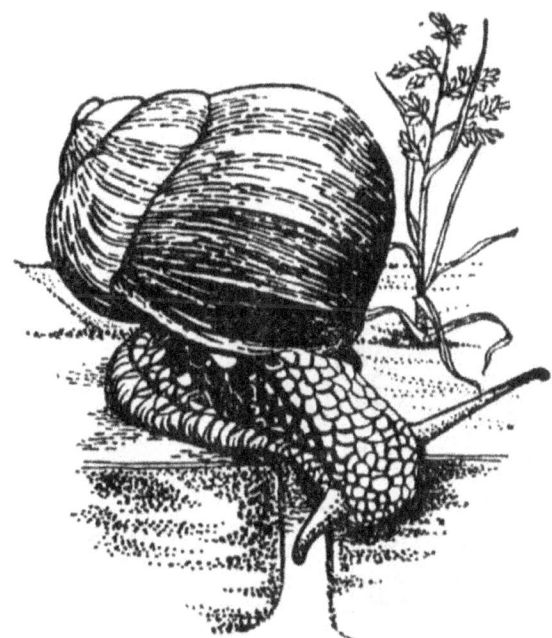

Snail upon the wall,
Have you got at all
Anything to tell
About your shell?

Only this, my child—
When the wind is wild,
Or when the sun is hot,
It's all I've got.

John Drinkwater

Poems to Enjoy, Book Three (5th edition)

THE VIPER

Barefoot I went and made no sound;
The earth was hot beneath:
The air was quivering around,
The circling kestrel eyed the ground
    And hung above the heath.

There in the pathway stretched along
The lovely serpent lay:
She reared not up the heath among,
She bowed her head, she sheathed her tongue,
    And shining stole away.

Fair was the brave embroidered dress,
Fairer the gold eyes shone:
Loving her not, yet I did bless
The fallen angel's comeliness;
And gazed when she had gone.

Ruth Pitter

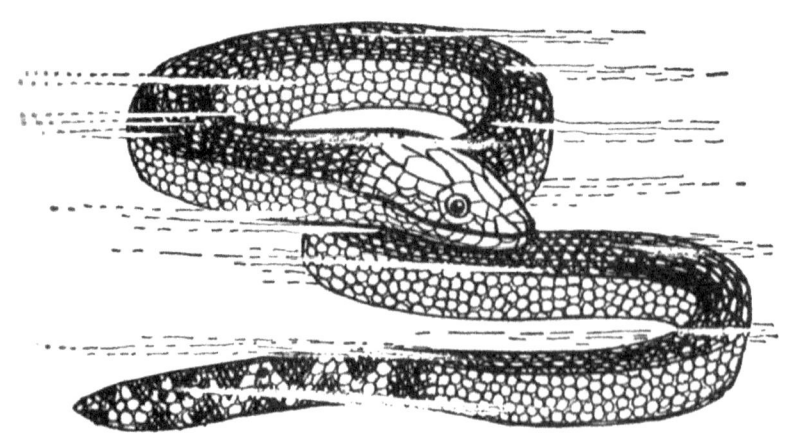

Poems to Enjoy, Book Three (5th edition)

THE SHIP

They have launched the little ship;
    She is riding by the quay;
Like a young doe to the river
    She has trembled to the sea.

Her sails are shaken loose,
    They flutter in the wind—
The cat's paws ripple round her
    And the gulls scream behind.

The rope is cast, she moves
    Daintily out and south,
Where the snarled ocean waits her
    With tiger-foaming mouth.

Richard Church

THE WATERHEN

At her step the water-hen
Springs from her nook, and skimming the clear stream,
    Ripples its waters in a sinuous curve,
    And dives again in safety.

Dante Gabriel Rossetti

Poems to Enjoy, Book Three (5th edition)

TO A BLACK GREYHOUND

Shining black in the shining light,
Inky black in the golden sun,
Graceful as the swallow's flight,
Light as swallow, wingèd one,
Swift as driven hurricane,
Double-sinewed stretch and spring,
Muddled thud of flying feet—
See the black dog galloping,
Hear his wild foot-beat.

See him lie when the day is dead,
Black curves curled on the boarded floor.
Sleep eyes, my sleepy-head—
Eyes that were aflame before.
Gentle now, they burn no more;
Gentle now and softly warm,
With the fire that made them bright
Hidden—as when after storm
Softly falls the night.

Julian Grenfell

Poems to Enjoy, Book Three (5th edition)

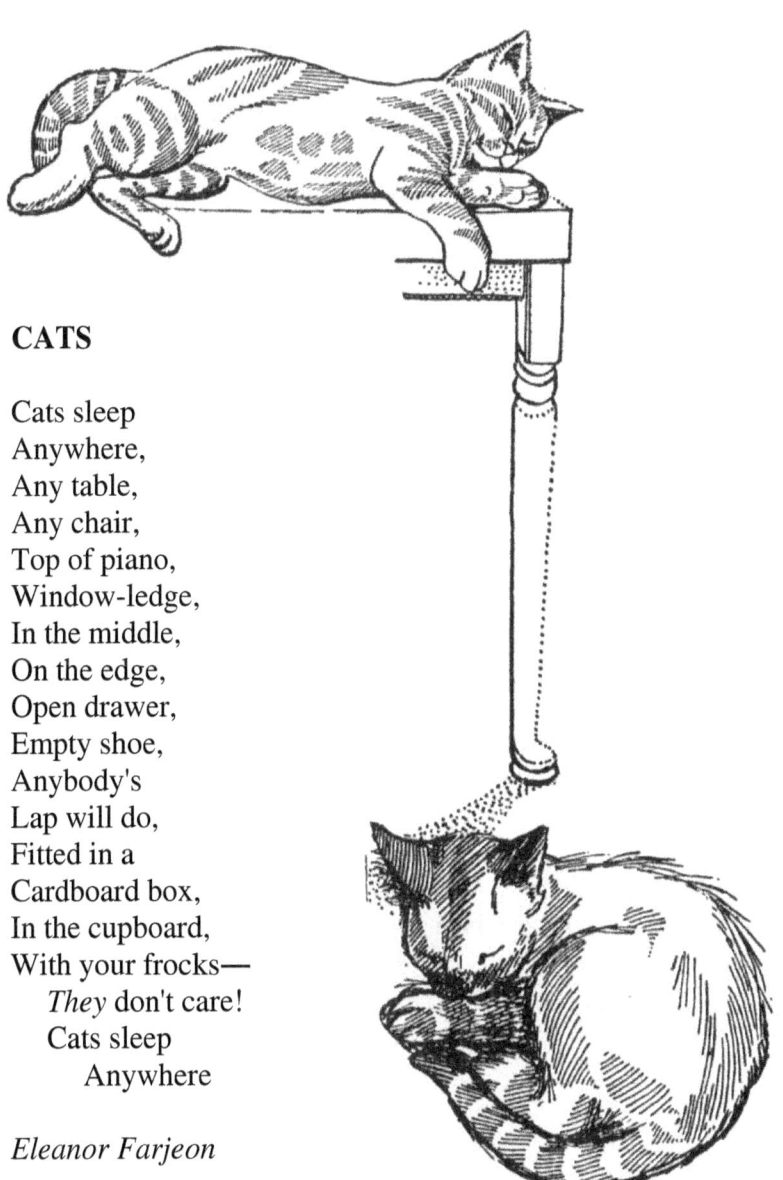

CATS

Cats sleep
Anywhere,
Any table,
Any chair,
Top of piano,
Window-ledge,
In the middle,
On the edge,
Open drawer,
Empty shoe,
Anybody's
Lap will do,
Fitted in a
Cardboard box,
In the cupboard,
With your frocks—
   They don't care!
  Cats sleep
    Anywhere

Eleanor Farjeon

Poems to Enjoy, Book Three (5th edition)

From *PAPER BOATS*

Day by day I float my paper boats one by one down the
    running stream.
In big black letters I write my name on them and the name of
    the village where I live.
I hope that someone in some strange land will find them and
    know who I am.
I load my little boats with *shiuli* flowers from our
Garden, and hope that these blooms of the
Dawn will be carried safely to land in the night.

Rabindranath Tagore

FLOOD

The lingering clouds, rolling, rolling,
And the settled rain, dripping, dripping,
In the Eight Directions—the same dusk.
The level lands—one great river.
Wine I have, wine I have:
Idly I drink at the eastern window.
Longingly—I think of my friends,
But neither boat nor carriage comes.

T'ao Ch'ien (Translated by *Arthur Waley*)

AN OLD SONG RE-SUNG

I saw a ship a-sailing, a-sailing, a-sailing,
With emeralds and rubies and sapphires in her hold;
And a bos'un in a blue coat bawling at the railing,
Piping through a silver call that had a chain of gold;
The summer wind was failing and the tall ship rolled.

I saw a ship a-steering, a-steering, a-steering,
With roses in red thread worked upon her sails;
With sacks of purple amethysts, the spoils of buccaneering,
Skins of musky yellow wine, and silks in bales,
His merry men were cheering, hauling on the brails.

I saw a ship a-sinking, a-sinking, a-sinking,
With glittering sea-water splashing on the decks,
With seamen in her spirit-room singing songs and drinking,
Pulling claret bottles down and knocking off the necks,
The broken glass was chinking as she sank among the wrecks.

John Masefield

Poems to Enjoy, Book Three (5th edition)

THE KRA

He runs along the branches, the kra,
He carries the fruit with him, the kra,
He runs to and fro, the kra;
Over the living bamboo, the kra,
Over the dead bamboo, the kra,
He runs along the branches, the kra,
He leaps about and screams, the kra,
He permits glimpses of himself, the kra,
He shows his grinning teeth, the kra.

Anon.

THE GALLANT SHIP

Upon the gale she stooped her side,
And bounded o'er the swelling tide,
    As she were dancing home;
The merry seamen laughed to see
Their gallant ship so lustily
    Furrow the sea-green foam.

Sir Walter Scott

A SPIKE OF GREEN

When I went out
The sun was hot
It shone upon
My flower pot.

And there I saw
A spike of green
That no one else
Had ever seen!

On other days
The things I see
Are mostly old
Except for me.

But this green spike
So new and small
Had never yet
Been seen at all!

Barbara Baker

Poems to Enjoy, Book Three (5th edition)

THE SHIP

There was no song nor shout of joy,
    Nor beam of moon or sun,
When she came back from the voyage
    Long ago begun;
But twilight on the waters
    Was quiet and grey,
And she glided steady, steady and pensive,
    Over the open bay.

Her sails were brown and ragged,
    And her crew hollow-eyed,
But their silent lips spoke content
    And their shoulders pride;
Though she had no captives on her deck,
    And in her hold
There were no heaps of corn and timber
    Or silks of gold.

Sir John Squire

THE AEROPLANE

Look at the aeroplane
   Up in the sky,
Seems like a giant lark
   Soaring on high.

See! on its outspread wing
   Flashes the light;
There sits the pilot brave
   Guiding its flight.

Hark! what a whirring song
   Comes from its throat,
Purr, purr of the engine,
   Its only note.

Now! high and higher yet,
   Upward it goes,
Till but a tiny speck
   'Gainst heaven it shows.

Oh! here it is again,
   Big as before,
Gracefully gliding down
   To earth once more.

Jeannie Kirby

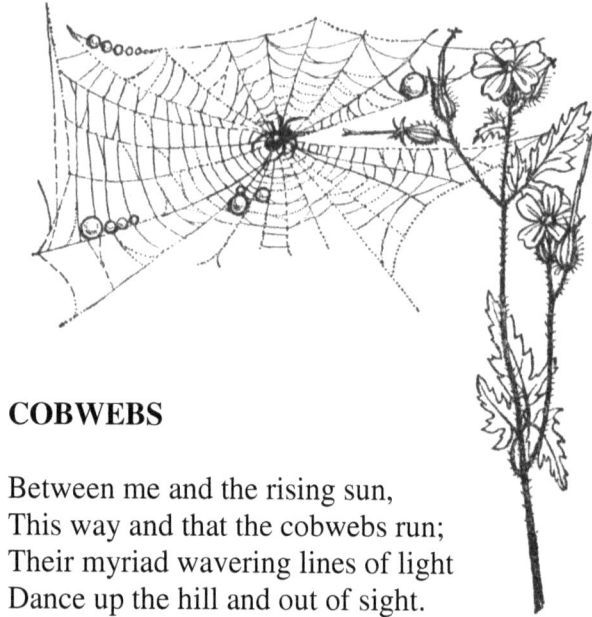

COBWEBS

Between me and the rising sun,
This way and that the cobwebs run;
Their myriad wavering lines of light
Dance up the hill and out of sight.

There is no land possesses half
So many lines of telegraph
As those the spider-elves have spun
Between me and the rising sun.

E.L.M. King

THE RIVALS

I heard a bird at dawn
    Singing sweetly on a tree,
That the dew was on the lawn,
    And the wind was on the lea;
But I didn't listen to him,
    For he didn't sing to me!

I didn't listen to him,
    For he didn't sing to me
That the dew was on the lawn,
And the wind was on the lea!
I was singing at the time,
    Just as prettily as he!

I was singing all the time,
    Just as prettily as he,
About the dew upon the lawn,
    And the wind upon the lea!
So I didn't listen to him,
    As he sang upon a tree!

James Stephens

Poems to Enjoy, Book Three (5th edition)

THE TRAIN

A green eye—and a red—in the dark,
Thunder—smoke—and a spark.

It is there—it is here—flashed by.
Whither will the wild thing fly?

It is rushing, tearing through the night,
Rending her gloom in its flight.

It shatters her silence with shrieks.
What is it the wild thing seeks?

Alas! for it hurries away
Them that are fain to stay.

Hurrah! for it carries home
Lovers and friends that roam.

Mary E. Coleridge

WHITE HORSES

Far out at sea
    There are horses to ride,
Little white horses
    That race with the tide.

Their tossing manes
    Are the white sea-foam,
And the lashing winds
    Are driving them home—

To shadowy stables
    Fast they must flee,
To the great green caverns
    Down under the sea.

Irene F. Pawsey

Poems to Enjoy, Book Three (5th edition)

THE CATERPILLAR

Brown and furry
Caterpillar in a hurry,
Take your walk
To the shady leaf, or stalk,
Or what not,
Which may be the chosen spot.
No toad spy you,
Hovering bird of prey pass by you;
Spin and die,
To live again a butterfly.

Christina Rossetti

THE CLIFF TOP

The cliff-top has a carpet
   Of lilac, gold and green:
The blue sky bounds the ocean,
   The white clouds scud between.

A flock of gulls are wheeling
   And wailing round my seat;
Above my head the heaven,
   The sea beneath my feet.

Robert Bridges

Poems to Enjoy, Book Three (5th edition)

THE LITTLE DANCERS

Lonely, save for a few faint stars, the sky
Dreams; and lonely, below, the little street
Into its gloom retires, secluded and shy.
Scarcely the dumb roar enters this soft retreat;
And all is dark, save where come flooding rays
From a tavern's window; there, to the brisk measure
Of an organ that down in an alley merrily plays,
Two children, all alone and no one by,
Holding their tattered frocks, thro' an airy maze
Of motion lightly threaded with nimble feet
Dance sedately, face to face they gaze,
Their eyes shining, grave with a perfect pleasure.

Lawrence Binyon

Part Three

A Tale is Told

Poems to Enjoy, Book Three (5th edition)

THE KING OF CHINA'S DAUGHTER

The King of China's daughter
So beautiful to see
With her face like yellow water, left
Her nutmeg tree.
Her little rope for skipping
She kissed and gave it me—
Made of painted notes of singing-birds
Among the fields of tea.
I skipped across the nutmeg grove,
I skipped across the sea;
But neither sun nor moon, my dear,
Has yet caught me.

The King of China's daughter,
She never would love me,
Though I hung my cap and bells upon
Her nutmeg tree.
For oranges and lemons,
The stars in bright blue air,
(I stole them long ago, my dear)
Were dangling there.

The Moon did give me silver pence,
The Sun did give me gold,
And both together softly blew,
And made my porridge cold;
But the King of China's daughter
Pretended not to see
When I hung my cap and bells upon
The nutmeg tree.

Edith Sitwell

IN YUNG-YANG

I was a child in Yung-Yang,
A little child I waved farewell.
After long years again I dwell
In world-forgotten Yung Yang.
Yet I recollect my play-time,
And in my dreams I see
The little ghosts of May-time
Waving farewell to me.

My father's house in Yung-Yang
Has fallen upon evil days.
No kinsmen o'er the crooked ways
Hail me as once in Yung-Yang.
No longer stands the old Moot-hall,
Gone is the market from the town;
The very hills have tumbled down
And stoned the valleys in their fall.

Only the waters of the Ch'in and Wei
Roll green and changeless as in days gone by.
Yet I recall my play-time,
And in my dreams I see
The little ghosts of May-time
Waving farewell to me.

Po Chu-i

Poems to Enjoy, Book Three (5th edition)

THE SHIP OF RIO

There was a ship of Rio
    Sailed out into the blue,
And nine and ninety monkeys
    Were all her jovial crew.
From bo'sun to the cabin boy,
    From quarter to caboose,
There weren't a stitch of calico
    To breech 'em—tight or loose;
From spar to deck. From deck to keel,
    From barnacle to shroud,
There weren't one pair of reach-me-downs
    To all that jabbering crowd.
But wasn't it a gladsome sight,
    When roared the deep-sea gales,
To see them reef her fore-and-aft,
    A-swinging by their tails!
Oh, wasn't it a gladsome sight,
    When glassy calm did come,
To see them squatting tailor-wise
    Around a keg of rum!
Oh, wasn't it a gladsome sight,
    When in she sailed to land,
To see them all a-scampering skip
    For nuts across the sand!

Walter de la Mare

Poems to Enjoy, Book Three (5th edition)

LAST POEM

They have put my bed beside the unpainted screen;
They have shifted my stove in front of the blue curtain.
I listen to my grandchildren, reading me a book;
I watch the servants, heating up my soup.
With rapid pencil I answer the poems of friends,
I feel in my pockets and pull out medicine-money.
When this superintendence of trifling affairs is done,
I lie back on my pillows and sleep with my face to the South.

Po Chu-i

Poems to Enjoy, Book Three (5th edition)

THE SNARE

I heard a sudden cry of pain!
    There is a rabbit in a snare:
Now I hear the cry again,
    But I cannot tell from where.

But I cannot tell from where
    He is calling out for aid;
Crying on the frightened air,
    Making everything afraid

Making everything afraid,
    Wrinkling up his little face,
As he cries again for aid;
    And I cannot find the place!

And I cannot find the place
    Where his paw is in the snare;
Little one! Oh, little one!
    I am searching everywhere.

James Stephens

THE LOST SHOE

Poor little Lucy
   By some mischance,
Lost her shoe
   As she did dance:
'Twas not on the stairs,
   Not in the hall;
Not where they sat
   At supper at all.
She looked in the garden,
   But there it was not;
Henhouse or kennel,
   Or high dovecote.
Dairy and meadow,
   And wild woods through
Showed not a trace
   Of Lucy's shoe.
Bird nor bunny
   Nor glimmering moon
Breathed a whisper
   Of where 'twas gone.
It was cried and cried,
   Oyez! Oyez!
In French, Dutch, Latin
   And Portuguese.
Ships the dark seas
   Went plunging through,
But none brought the news
   Of Lucy's shoe;

Poems to Enjoy, Book Three (5th edition)

And still she patters
   In silk and leather,
O'er snow, sand, shingle,
   In every weather;
Spain, and Africa,
   Hindustan,
Java, China,
   And lamped Japan,
Plain and desert.
   She hops—hops through,
Pernambuco
   To gold Peru;
Mountain and forest,
   And river too,
All the world over
   For her lost shoe.

Walter de la Mare

OH! CRUEL WERE MY PARIENTS

Oh! cruel were my parients as tore my love from me,
And cruel was the Press Gang as took him off to sea,
And cruel was the little boat as rowed him from the strand,
And cruel was the big ship as sailed him from the land.
Sing too rol lol, too rol lol fay.

Ah! cruel was the water as bore her love from Mary.
And cruel was the fair wind as wouldn't blow contrary,
And cruel was the Captain, and the boatswain and the men
As didn't care a farthing if we never met again.
    Sing too rol lol, too rol lol fay.

Anon.

Poems to Enjoy, Book Three (5th edition)

I KEEP SIX HONEST SERVING-MEN

I keep six honest serving men,
    (They taught me all I knew);
Their names are What and Why and When
    And How and Where and Who.
I send them over land and sea,
    I send them east and west;
But after they have worked for me,
    I give them all a rest.

I let them rest from nine till five,
    For I am busy then,
As well as breakfast, lunch and tea,
    For they are hungry men:
But different folk have different views;
    I know a person small—
She keeps ten million serving-men,
    Who get no rest at all!

She sends 'em abroad on her own affairs,
    From the second she opens her eyes—
One million Hows, two million Wheres,
    And seven million Whys!

Rudyard Kipling

THE SEVEN FIDDLERS

A blue robe on their shoulder,
    And an ivory bow in hand,
Seven fiddlers came with their fiddles
    A-fiddling through the land,
And they fiddled a tune on their fiddles
    That none could understand.

For none who heard their fiddling
    Might keep his ten toes still,
E'en the cripple threw down his crutches,
    And danced against his will:
Young and old they all fell a-dancing,
    While the fiddlers fiddled their fill.

Poems to Enjoy, Book Three (5th edition)

They fiddled down to the ferry—
The ferry by Severn-side,
And they stepped aboard the ferry,
   None else to row or guide,
And deftly steered the pilot,
   And stoutly the oars they plied.

Then suddenly in mid-channel
   These fiddlers ceased to row,
And the pilot spake to his fellow
   In a tongue that none may know:
"Let us home to our fathers and brothers,
   And the maidens we love below."

Then the fiddlers seized their fiddles,
   And sang to their fiddles a song:
"We are coming, coming, O brothers,
   To the home we have left so long,
For the world still loves the fiddler,
   And the fiddler's tune is strong."

Then they stept from out the ferry
   Into the Severn-Sea,
Down into the depths of the waters
   Where the homes of the fiddlers be,
And the ferry boat drifted slowly
   Forth to the ocean free!

But where those jolly fiddlers
   Walked down into the deep,
The ripples are never quiet,
   But for ever dance and leap,
Though the Severn-Sea be silent,
   And the winds be all asleep.
               Sebastian Evans

SOLDIER, WON'T YOU MARRY ME?

Soldier, soldier, won't you marry me?
It's O a fife and drum.
How can I marry such a pretty girl as you
When I've got no hat to put on?

Off to the tailor she did go
As hard as she could run,
Brought him back the finest was there.
Now, soldier, put it on.

Soldier, soldier, won't you marry me?
It's O a fife and drum.
How can I marry such a pretty girl as you
When I've got no coat to put on?

Off to the tailor she did go
As hard as she could run,
Brought him back the finest was there.
Now, soldier, put it on.

Soldier, soldier, won't you marry me?
It's O a fife and drum.
How can I marry such a pretty girl as you
When I've got no shoes to put on?

Off to the shoe shop she did go
As hard as she could run,
Brought him back the finest was there.
Now, soldier, put them on.

Poems to Enjoy, Book Three (5th edition)

Soldier, soldier, won't you marry me?
It's O a fife and drum.
How can I marry such as pretty girl as you
With a wife and baby at home?

Anon.

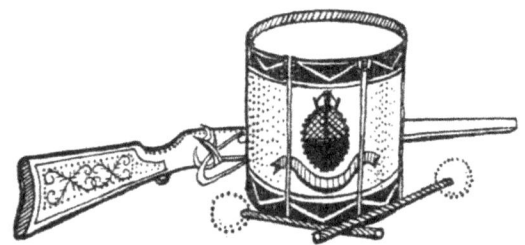

THE FISHER'S WIDOW

The boats go out and the boats come in
    Under the wintry sky;
And the rain and foam are white in the wind,
    And the white gulls cry.

She sees the sea, when the wind is wild,
    Swept by the windy rain;
And her heart's a-weary of sea and land
    As the long days wane.

She sees the torn sails fly in the foam,
    Broad on the sky-line grey;
And the boats go out and the boats come in,
    But there's one away.

Arthur Symons

Poems to Enjoy, Book Three (5th edition)

Song from THE FLOWER OF OLD JAPAN

We sailed across the silver seas
   And saw the sea-blue bowers,
We saw the purple cherry trees,
And all the foreign flowers,
We travelled in a palanquin
   Beyond the caravan,
And yet our hearts had never seen
   The Flower of Old Japan.

The Flower above all other flowers,
   The Flower that never dies,
Before whose throne the scented hours
   Offer their sacrifice,
The Flower that here on earth below
Reveals the heavenly plan;
But only little children know
   The Flower of Old Japan.

Alfred Noyes

THE NIGHTJAR

We loved our Nightjar, but she would not stay with us.
We had found her lying as dead, but soft and warm,
Under the apple tree beside the old thatched wall.
Two days we kept her in a basket by the fire,
Fed her, and thought she might well live—till suddenly
In the very moment of most confiding hope
She raised herself all tense, quivered and drooped and died.
Tears sprang into my eyes—why not? The heart of man
Soon sets itself to love a living companion,
The more so if by chance it asks some care of him.
And this one had the kind of loveliness that goes
Far deeper than the optic nerve—full fathom five
To the soul's ocean cave, where Wonder and Reason
Tell their alternate dreams of how the world was made.
So wonderful she was—her wings the wings of night
But powdered here and there with tiny golden clouds
And wave-like markings like sea-ripples on the sand.
O how I wish I might never forget that bird—
Never!—but even now, like all beauty of earth,
She is fading from me into the dusk of Time.

Sir Henry Newbolt

Poems to Enjoy, Book Three (5th edition)

THE UPSIDE-DOWN WORLD

I know a place that holds the sky,
A place where little white clouds lie;
The edge is all as green as grass,
The middle is as smooth as glass;
And there the round sun makes his bed;
And there a tree stands on its head;
Sometimes a bird sits in that tree;
Sometimes it sings a song to me;

And always in that shining place
I see a little shining face;
She nods and smiles; but all the same
The girl down there won't tell her name.

Hamish Hendry

Poems to Enjoy, Book Three(5th edition)

THE HAG

The hag is astride
This night for to ride,
The devil and she together;
Through thick and through thin,
Now out and then in,
Though ne'er so foul be the weather.

A thorn or a burr
She takes for a spur,
With a lash of a bramble she rides now;
Through brakes and through briars,
Oe'r ditches and mires,
She follows the spirit that guides now.

No beast for his food
Dare now range the wood,
But hushed in his lair he lies lurking;
While mischiefs by these,
On land and on seas,
At noon of night are a-working

The storm will arise
And trouble the skies;
This night, and more for the wonder,
The ghost from the tomb,
Affrighted shall come,
Called out by the clap of the thunder.

Robert Herrick

Poems to Enjoy, Book Three (5th edition)

THE SILVER ROAD

Last night I saw a Silver Road
    Go straight across the Sea;
And quick as I raced along the Shore,
    That quick Road followed me.

It followed me all round the Bay,
    Where small Waves danced in tune;
And at the end of the Silver Road,
    There hung a Silver Moon.

A large round Moon on a pale green Sky,
    With a pathway bright and broad;
Some night I shall bring that Silver Moon
    Across that Silver Road!

Hamish Hendry

THE BALLAD OF EARL HALDAN'S DAUGHTER

It was Earl Haldan's daughter,
   She looked across the sea;
She looked across the water;
   And long and loud laughed she:
"The locks of six princesses
   Must be my marriage fee,
So hey bonny boat, and ho bonny boat!
   Who comes a-wooing me?"

It was Earl Haldan's daughter,
   She walked along the sand;
When she was aware of a knight so fair,
   Came sailing to the land.
His sails were all of velvet,
   His mast of beaten gold,
And "Hey bonny boat and ho bonny boat!
   Who saileth here so bold?"

"The locks of five princesses
   I won beyond the sea;
I clipt their golden tresses,
   To fringe a cloak for thee.
One handful yet is wanting,
   But one of all the tale;

Poems to Enjoy, Book Three (5th edition)

So hey bonny boat, and ho bonny boat!
    Furl up they velvet sail!"

He leapt into the water,
    That rover young and bold,
He gript Earl Haldan's daughter,
    He clipt her locks of gold:
"Go weep, go weep, proud maiden,
    The tale is full today,
Now hey bonny boat, and ho bonny boat!
    Sail westward ho! Away!"

Charles Kingsley

TARTARY

If I were Lord of Tartary.
    Myself and me alone,
My bed should be of ivory,
    Of beaten gold my throne;
And in my court should peacocks flaunt,
And in my forests tigers haunt,
And in my pools great fishes slant
    Their fins athwart the sun.

If I were Lord of Tartary,
    Trumpeters every day
To every meal should summon me,
    And in my courtyard bray;
And in the evenings lamps would shine
Yellow as honey, red as wine,
While harp and flute and mandoline,
    Made music sweet and gay.

If I were Lord of Tartary,
   I'd wear a rope of beads,
White, and gold, and green they'd be—
   And clustered thick as seeds;
And ere should wane the morning star,
I'd don my robe and scimitar,
And zebras seven should draw my car
   Through Tartary's dark glades.

Lord of the fruits of Tartary,
   Her rivers silver-pale!
Lord of the hills of Tartary,
   Glen, thicket, wood and dale!
Her flashing stars, her scented breeze,
Her trembling lakes, like foamless seas,
Her bird-delighting citron-trees
   In every purple vale!

Walter de la Mare

Poems to Enjoy, Book Three (5th edition)

ELDORADO

Gaily bedight,
A gallant knight,
In sunshine and in shadow,
Had journeyed along,
Singing a song,
In search of Eldorado.

But he grew old—
This knight so bold—
And o'er his heart a shadow
Fell as he found
No spot of ground
That looked like Eldorado.

And, as his strength
Failed him at length,
He met a pilgrim shadow:
"Shadow," said he,
"Where can it be,
This land of Eldorado?"

"Over the mountains
Of the Moon,
Down the valley of the Shadow,
Ride, boldly ride,"
The shade replied,
"If you seek for Eldorado."

Edgar Allan Poe

THE LION

The lion walks behind his bars,
His tawny shoulders ebb and flow,
With swaying flank and lowered mane
He pads the asphalt, proud and slow.

If he could break his rusted cage,
How many eyes would open wide
To see him flaming through the gap,
A lion springing in his pride!

But now he walks with silent tread,
Swinging and turning in his den,
He yawns, and blinks his golden eyes
Above the prying sons of men.

Herbert Asquith

Poems to Enjoy, Book Three (5th edition)

HIAWATHA'S CHILDHOOD

At the door on Summer evenings
Sat the little Hiawatha;
Heard the whispering of the pine-trees,
Heard the lapping of the waters,
Sounds of music, words of wonder;
"Minne-wawa!" said the pine trees,
"Mudway-aushka!" said the water.
Saw the fire-fly, Wah-wah-taysee,
Flitting through the dusk of evening,
With the twinkle of its candle
Lighting up the brakes and bushes,
And he sang the song of children,
Sang the song Nokomis taught him:
"Wah-wah-taysee, little fire-fly,
Little, flitting, white-fire insect,
Little, dancing, white-fire creature,
Light me with your little candle,
Ere upon my bed I lay me,
Ere in sleep I close my eyelids!"
Saw the moon rise from the water
Rippling, rounding from the water,
Saw the flecks and shadows on it,
Whispered, "What is that, Nokomis?"
And the good Nokomis answered:
"Once a warrior, very angry,
Seized his grandmother, and threw her
Up into the sky at midnight;
Right against the moon he threw her;
'Tis her body that you see there."
Saw the rainbow in the heaven,
In the eastern sky, the rainbow,
Whispered, "What is that, Nokomis?"
And the good Nokomis answered:

"'Tis the heaven of flowers you see there;
All the wild flowers of the forest,
All the lilies of the prairie,
When on earth they fade and perish,
Blossom in the heaven above us."

H.W. Longfellow

Poems to Enjoy, Book Three (5th edition)

WANDER-THIRST

Beyond the East the Sunrise; beyond the West the sea;
And East and West the Wander-Thirst that will not let me be;
It works in me like madness, dear, to bid me say goodbye,
For the seas call, and the stars call, and, oh! The call of the sky!

I know not where the white road runs, nor what the blue hills are,
But a man can have the sun for a friend, and for his guide a star;
And there's no end of voyaging when once the voice is heard,
For the rivers call, and the road calls, and oh! the call of a bird!

Yonder the long horizon lies, and there by night and by day
The old ships draw to home again, the young ships sail away;
And come I may, but go I must, and if men ask you why,
You can put the blame on the stars and the sun and the white road and the sky.

Gerald Gould

THE MINSTREL BOY

The Minstrel Boy to the war is gone,
In the ranks of death you'll find him;
His father's sword he has girded on,
And his wild harp slung behind him.
"Land of song!" said the warrior-bard,
"Though all the world betrays thee,
One sword at least, thy rights shall guard,
One faithful harp shall praise thee!"

The Minstrel fell!—but the foeman's chain
Could not bring his proud soul under;
The harp he loved ne'er spoke again,
For he tore its cords asunder;
And said, "No chains shall sully thee,
Thou soul of love and bravery!
Thy songs were made for the pure and free:
They shall never sound in slavery!"

Thomas Moore

Poems to Enjoy, Book Three (5th edition)

THE EMPEROR OF CHINA

The Emperor of China,
   High upon his throne
Of sandalwood and ivory
   And dark blood-stone,
Canopied in tissue
   Of purest, palest gold,
Embroidered with flashing jewels
   Of worth untold,
Pouted up his lips and said,
   "Tonight I will dine
On song-birds' hearts and tongues
   Pickled in sweet wine."

A nightingale of China
   With wild free song
Hung the fragrant air with bells
   All night long.
In the palace garden
   On a willow tree,

Little bird in brown coat
Singing endlessly;
Singing to the scarlet flowers,
　　Singing ever yet—
Silently the hunters
　　Slink up with their net.

The Emperor of China,
　　Pouting as he dines,
Picks and pecks among the plates,
Dips into the wines;
Savours from a dish of tongues
And hearts of singing birds,
Pushes it away from him
　　With listless, pouting words.
"Too sweet. Too spiced." And languidly
　　Raises to his lips
A golden cup of golden tea.
　　And tries, and tastes, and sips.

In the palace garden
　　By the scarlet flowers,
All is still and lonely
　　Through the long night hours;
On the yellow willow,
　　The weeping willow tree,
No small bird in brown coat,
　　Singing endlessly.
Silence wraps the scarlet flowers,
　　Sweeps the flowery dells—
No nightingale of China
　　To hang the air with bells.

Mary Daunt

Poems to Enjoy, Book Three (5th edition)

DOWN OUR STREET

Down our street when I was a boy I met with a friendly man
Who took me to the stone-cross steps and said to me, "See Japan."

I stared at the East he pointed; never have I seen a sky so fine,
A shining height of clouds sun-bright, and loftier hyaline.

And, "See the Mountain," said my friend, and I traced the region cloud,
With intense wish to shape that peak, which made his smile so proud.

I nearly saw not that alone, but as it felt to me
Cities and domes and lakes and falls and even doorway and tree.

But just the final face of the thing came not; and I told him so,
I only knew that the man was right and that I was stupid and slow.

He smiled, and said I should find all out, and the words he left me were these:
"I come from my shop to see Japan, and the Mountain, when I please."

Edmund Blunden

MILK FOR THE CAT

When the tea is brought at five o'clock,
And all the neat curtains are drawn with care,
The little black cat with bright green eyes
Is suddenly purring there.

At first she pretends, having nothing to do,
She has come in merely to blink by the grate,
But though tea may be late or the milk may be sour,
She is never late.

And presently her agate eyes
Take a soft, large, milky haze,
And her independent casual glance
Becomes a stiff hard gaze.

Then she stamps her claws or lifts her ears
Or twists her tail and begins to stir,
Till suddenly all her little body becomes
One breathing trembling purr.

The children eat and wriggle and laugh;
The two old ladies stroke their silk:
But the cat is grown small and thin with desire,
Transformed to a creeping lust for milk.

The white saucer like some full moon descends
At last from the clouds of the table above;
She sighs and dreams and thrills and glows,
Transfigured with love.

She nestles over the shining rim,
Buries her chin in the creamy sea;
Her tail hangs loose; each drowsy paw
Is doubled under each bending knee.

A long dim ecstasy holds her life;
Her world is an infinite shapeless white,
Till her tongue has curled the last holy drop,
Then she sinks back into the night,

Draws and dips her body to heap
Her sleepy nerves in the great arm-chair,
Lies defeated and buried deep
Three or four hours unconscious there.

Harold Monro

UP AND AWAY

If ever I travel to France or Spain,
I mean go in an aeroplane.

I've read all about it, and now I know
How they swing the propeller, and off you go!
A run and a bounce, and you're looking down
From high in the sky on a little toy town;
And the fields like a bedspread, green and brown.
With ribbony roads all winding through,
So empty and quiet, it hardly seems true
That anyone's there looking up to see
You racing along, like a big letter T,
Through the clouds and into the light,
Smaller and smaller, and out of sight.
And the aeroplane climbs and dips and swings
While loudly and proudly the engine sings,
And the pilot sits in his cockpit there,
With the wireless to bring him the news of the air.

Poems to Enjoy, Book Three (5th edition)

Then all of a sudden beneath you there'll be
The tiny ships on the shiny sea,
And next you're Abroad—and I hope it seems
Just as lovely as in your dreams,
With castles, cathedrals, and cities with walls,
Forests and fountains and waterfalls,
Great grim mountains all rocks and snow,
And broad, bright rivers away below,
Till, tired of the sky, like a bird coming home,
With a dive you arrive at the aerodrome.

It might be horrid in fog or rain,
But I mean to go in an aeroplane
If ever I travel to France or Spain.

T. Mark

TWO RED ROSES ACROSS THE MOON

There was a lady lived in a hall,
Large of eyes and slim and tall;
And ever she sang from noon to noon,
"Two red roses across the moon."

There was a knight came riding by
In early spring, when the roads were dry;
And he heard that lady sing at the noon,
"Two red roses across the moon."

Yet none the more he stopped at all,
But he rode a-gallop past the hall;
And left that lady singing at noon,
"Two red roses across the moon."

Because, forsooth, the battle was set,
And the scarlet and gold had got to be met,
He rode on the spur till the next warm noon;
Two red roses across the moon.

But the battle was scattered from hill to hill,
From the windmill to the watermill;
And he said to himself, as it neared the noon,
"Two red roses across the moon."

You scarce could see for the scarlet and blue,
A golden helm or a golden shoe;
So he cried, as the fight grew thick at the noon,
"Two red roses across the moon."

Poems to Enjoy, Book Three (5th edition)

Verily then the gold bore through
The huddled spears of the scarlet and blue;
And they cried, as they cut them down at the noon,
"Two red roses across the moon."

I trow he stooped when he rode again
By the hall, though draggled sore with the rain;
And his lips were pinched to kiss at the noon
Two red roses across the moon.

Under the may she stopped to the crown,
All was gold, there was nothing of brown,
And the horns blew up in the hall at noon,
Two red roses across the moon.

William Morris

BOOT AND SADDLE

Boot, saddle, to horse, and away!
Rescue my Castle, before the hot day
Brightens to blue from its silvery grey,
   Boot, saddle, to horse, and away.

Ride past the suburbs, asleep as you'd say;
Many's the friend there, will listen and pray
"God's luck to gallants that strike up the lay—
   Boot, saddle, to horse and away."

Forty miles off, like a roebuck at bay,
Flouts Castle Brancepeth the Roundheads' array:
Who laughs "Good fellows, ere this, by my fay,
   Boot, saddle, to horse, and away"?

Who? My wife Gertrude; that honest and gay,
Laughs when you talk of surrendering, "Nay!
I've better counsellors; what counsel they?
   Boot, saddle, to horse, and away!

Robert Browning

Poems to Enjoy, Book Three (5th edition)

TEACHING AND LEARNING NOTES AND GUIDE

NOTE: *When explanations of words and phrases are given, these refer to the meanings within the context of each particular poem. In other contexts, they may have other meanings.*

The Explanations are given in the order in which the words and phrases occur in the poem concerned.

Explanation of Selected Terms

The following are explanations of selected terms which readers will come across in this book.

Sonnet
A sonnet is a poem of fourteen decasyllabic lines (ten syllables per line) or, rarely, octosyllabic (eight syllables per line) lines. Sonnets can be composed of an octave (eight lines) expressing one phase of an idea, and a sestet (six lines) expressing another phase of the same idea. There are several other types of sonnet form.

Ballad
A ballad is a poem or song which tells a story, usually in short stanzas (verses) and often with a refrain (a phrase repeated at intervals, usually at the end of each stanza).

Rhyme
Similar sounds in two or more words, especially at the ends of lines of poetry.

Traditional
Something (usually knowledge) which is passed from generation to generation.

Poems to Enjoy, Book Three (5th edition)

PART ONE: POEMS TO SPEAK

THE SPIDER AND THE FLY (*Page* 18)
Individual students can take turns to speak the parts of the Spider and the Fly. The single narrative lines (e.g. 'Said the spider to the fly'; 'Said the little fly', etc.) may be spoken by the rest of the class in chorus, whilst the teacher takes the more extended passages.

RIKKI-TIKKI-TAVI (*Page* 21)
Some preliminary discussion should take place before this poem is read, to ensure that the students know something about the habits and appearance of a mongoose and of a cobra. A reading might then follow. The teacher could speak the first three lines of verse one, and one student could speak line 4. In verse two the teacher could say lines 1 and 3, whilst the whole class speaks lines 2 and 4 in chorus. A similar arrangement could be used for the last verse. A feeling of tense, expectant excitement should be encouraged in the reading to add to the impression of two adversaries face-to-face, each seeking for an opening to strike at the other.

THE STORY OF JOHNNY HEAD-IN-AIR (*Page* 22)
This poem can be used for choral work. The whole of verse one, for example, can be spoken by the teacher, except for the last two lines, which can be taken by the whole class. Verse two may be given to one individual student, but the last line can be said by a small group. The third verse can be spoken by all the students; verse four by another individual student; verse five can be a solo by a third student; verse six a solo by the teacher; the first six lines of verse seven can be said by the small group, and the other lines of the last verse may be taken by the whole class. Many other variations are, of course, possible at the teacher's discretion.

VOCABULARY
trudged: walked along with some effort.

N.B. The words, 'Johnny Head-in-Air' were used during the Second World War by the poet, John Pudney, in his rather sad poem, "For Johnny." It begins:
    Do not despair for Johnny Head in Air.
    He sleeps as sound as Johnny Underground..."

Poems to Enjoy, Book Three (5th edition)

WILL YOU WALK A LITTLE FASTER? (*Page* 24)
One student can say the whiting's lines ('said a whiting to a snail' in the first line may be spoken by the teacher) and the whole class can speak the two 'will you, won't you', lines at the end of the first verse. After the whiting has spoken again in verse two, the teacher might say the narrative phrases, 'But the snail replied'; 'and gave a look askance', whilst another soloist repeats the snail's lines. The 'would not, could not', lines might be taken by the whole class. This pattern can be repeated in verse three.

THE COBBLERS' SONG (*Page* 26)
After a preliminary reading by the teacher, the students could be asked to suggest suitable groupings for reading aloud. This is good practice and students feel an added sense of accomplishment when their suggestions are discussed by the teacher and class and eventually adopted, rehearsed and performed.

FROM THE FIREMAN'S BALL (*Page* 27)
For more advanced choral work. Many variations are possible. For a class with previous experience of solo and group reading one possible approach is as follows: Lines 1 and 2, whole class in chorus; lines 3-10, a small group; lines 11 and 12, the whole class in chorus; line 13, soloist; line 14, soloist; line 15, 'clear the street', soloist and 'Boom, boom', the whole class. Line 16, half the class; line 17, all the class; line 18, half the class; lines 19 and 20, all the class; lines 21-24, soloist; lines 25-26, a small group; lines 27-28, soloist; line 29 ('tis the') small group; line 30, the whole class, loudly; line 31, small group; line 32, small group; line 33, the whole class, loudly; line 34, small group; line 35, small group; lines 36-37, the whole class; lines 38-39, small group; lines 40, 41 and 42 by different soloists; lines 43-45 can be spoken by the whole class, adding speed as each line is read. Line 46 can be taken by the small group, observing the pauses indicated and the whole class might speak the last line ('Of the firemen's ball') as a grand climax. After practice spread over a number of lessons, the teacher can experiment with 'light', 'medium', and 'heavy' voices in the small group.

Poems to Enjoy, Book Three (5th edition)

SONG OF THE GRACES (*Page* 29)
Suitable for a girls' or mixed class. A group of six or seven girls could be asked to speak lines 1-4 in the first verse, and the whole class could say the chorus. For the rest of the poem, lines 1 and 3 in each verse could be said by different soloists, whilst the class repeats the refrain.
VOCABULARY
Nimming: picking.

ANTHONY WASHED HIS FACE TODAY (*Page* 31)
This poem, suitable for most fifth year classes, lends itself to dramatization. Four students (Anthony, Rose, Mother and Father) can mime the story whilst choral speaking of the poem accompanies the mime. A suitable choral arrangement might be:
Verse One:
Line 1—soloist (in surprised tone).
Line 3 — soloist (still surprised).
Lines 2 and 4—the whole class.
Verse Two:
Lines 1, 2, and 3—soloist (puzzled).
Line 4—the whole class.
Verse Three:
Lines 1 and 3—soloist (surprised).
Line 2—the whole class (sternly and seriously).
Line 4—the whole class (wonderingly).
Verse 4:
Lines 1 and 2 — soloist (amazed).
Lines 3 and 4 — the whole class (worriedly).

BEE-SONG (*Page* 32)
This poem provides practice of the sibilant consonant, 'z.' The whole class could say line 1; lines 2, 3 and 4 could be spoken by a small group. The whole class again could take line 5. Lines 6 and 7 could be solos; the class could say line 8, and lines 9 and 10 could be spoken by the small group.
VOCABULARY
leese: lose

Poems to Enjoy, Book Three (5th edition)

WHEN CATS RUN HOME (*Page* 32)
For practice of 'w' and ə (*ir* as in 'bird') three separate groups can be selected from the class. Group A could say line 1, Group B, line 2, and Group C, line 3. Groups A and B together might say the fourth and fifth lines, whilst all the students in the class speak the last two lines of the poem.

WHILE GOING THE ROAD (*Page* 33)
A lively poem suitable for solo, group and chorus work. In the first verse, lines, 1, 3, 5, 6, and 7 can be taken by a soloist and line 8 by a different soloist. The chorus which appears in full in the first verse (lines 9-12), can be said by the same or by different small groups throughout. In the other verses, the soloists remain the same. Lines 1 and 3 ('Hurroo! Hurroo!) of each verse can be spoken by the whole class.
VOCABULARY
Och: Oh!
took leg bail: ran away from me (*leg bail* = legal term for escape from custody by flight)
Beau: sweetheart.

THE MONKEY SAILORS (*Page* 36)
Good practice for ɔə (*aw* as in 'law'), 'i:' (*ee* as in 'meet', 'seat) and æ (as in 'sat').
An interesting poem for varied choral arrangements. Lines 1 and 2 could be said by two separate soloists; line 3 could be spoken by the whole class in chorus; lines 4 and 5 could be said solo; lines 6, 7 and 8 could be taken by the chorus; line 9 could be a solo and line 10 could be spoken as a duet. The four separate words in lines 11 and 12 could be taken by four groups. Lines 13 and 14 could be spoken by the soloists, line 15 by a group and the last three lines of the poem by the class in chorus.

THE CLOTHES-LINE (*Page* 37)
For group and chorus work with the teacher. The first two lines may be said by the teacher; lines 3 and 4 can be spoken by the whole class; two separate groups might take lines 5 and 6; lines 7 and 8 are suitable for two soloists, and the teacher can follow with lines 9 and 10. The groups can speak lines 11 and 12; the teacher, line 13; the whole class line 14, and the teacher the last four lines.

Poems to Enjoy, Book Three (5th edition)

THE PLAINT OF THE CAMEL (*Page* 38)
The first four lines of each stanza can be spoken by four separate soloists; the last three lines can be taken as a chorus by the whole class, or by five different groups.

DUCKS' DITTY (*Page* 40)
The first three lines of each verse could be taken by three soloists; the last line of each verse by separate groups or by the whole class in chorus.
VOCABULARY: ditty: song.
backwater: still water which has come from a nearby stream.
rushes: marsh plants with long, thin stems.
roach: fresh-water fish.
dabbling: playing with the feet, or bill, in water.

THE TWELVE DAYS OF CHRISTMAS (*Page* 41)
To be said and, if possible, sung by the whole class together.

THE DEAF WOMAN (*Page* 42)
Two students can mime the action of this poem whilst it is being read. There can be a different soloist for each line of the poem, or as many students as possible might be given a chance to speak the questioner's and the old woman's lines during the course of the lesson.

ECHO (*Page* 43)
The questions 'Who called?' and 'Who cares?' can be said by all the students in the class as the teacher speaks the rest of the poem. Questions and a discussion should follow. Questions which stimulate the imagination will help the students to reach towards the meaning, for example:
 1. You are in the woods with the poet. What do you hear?
 2. What do you see?
 3. What do you feel?

VOCABULARY: baffled: puzzled, perplexed.
brake: small thicket of trees.
For mockery's sake: making a fool of the poet.

Poems to Enjoy, Book Three (5th edition)

TURTLE SOUP (*Page* 44)
Lines 1-3 may be taken by a soloist; lines 4 and 5 by a small group; lines 6 and 7 by the whole class; line 8 by the group and line 9 again by the whole class in chorus. In the second verse, lines 1 and 2 can be spoken by a soloist, lines 3, 4 and 5 by the group; lines 6, 7 and 9 by the whole class, and line 8 by the group.
VOCABULARY
tureen: a deep dish, often used to hold soup.

THE DANCING CABMAN (*Page* 45)
Although this is an amusing poem, the effect is added to if it is spoken with complete seriousness. The whole of the poem can be said by a selected group from the class. The rest of the class can be kept in the lesson by being asked to make suggestions for the arrangement of the poem and by being a critical audience. It is suggested that the first line should be taken slowly, with attention being paid to the '*l*' sounds. Line 2 in the first verse can be said briskly; in line 3 the slow '*d*' sounds should be observed; line 4 can be brisk; lines 5 and 6 important, and lines 7 and 8, sad. In lines 9 and 10 the '*l*' sounds need care, and the last two lines of the first verse might be said incredulously. In verse 2, lines 1, 3 and 4 can be brisk; line 2, slower; lines 5 and 6, 'skimmingly' and light; lines 7 and 8 might be very slow with a pause after 'face.' Line 9 can be quicker; line 10 dainty; liner 11 slow and ponderous, and the last line of the poem, brisk again.

EARLY IN THE MORNING (*Page* 46)
The four lines of each verse can be spoken by soloists or separate groups, whilst the refrain can be said by the whole class in chorus. (The refrain is given entire at the end of the first verse. For all other verses, it is represented by "etc.". Similarly, the opening line in each verse is repeated twice. In the first verse, all three lines are given. For all other verses, lines 2 and 3 are represented by "etc." When reciting this poem, "etc." of course is not spoken; but the lines indicated are said in full.)
If the words can be sung to the well-known tune, so much the better.
VOCABULARY
scuppers: drains in the side of a ship at deck level to remove water coming over the side.
up she rises: the pitching motion of a ship.
taffrail: the rail around the stern of a ship.
running bowline: a type of knot; *yard-arm*: either end of a sail.

129

Poems to Enjoy, Book Three (5th edition)

LONE DOG (*Page* 47)
Each of the lines in verses one and two can be taken by individual students. In verse three, it is suggested that lines 1 and 3 be taken by a group, and lines 2 and 4 by the whole class in chorus.
VOCABULARY
bay the moon: to howl at the moon.
cringing: cowering, behaving with exaggerated politeness.

THE DROP OF WATER (*Page* 47)
The first line can be said solo and lines 2 and 3 by the whole class together. The one-word lines throughout the poem might be taken by different soloists or separate groups; the lines 11-15 can be spoken by the whole class; lines 18-23 can be said by a group; lines 24 and 25 by the whole class, and lines 28-37 by the teacher. There is good practice of the sound 'sh' as in 'shut' in line 2, and initial and final consonants can be practised throughout.

SIR EGLAMORE (*Page* 49)
The teacher can tell the story, whilst all the class says the chorus lines ('Fa la lanky down dilly').
VOCABULARY
plaguey hard hide: very hard skin.
the strongest steel abide: could bear the strongest steel.
eke: also.

THE MARRIAGE OF THE FROG AND THE MOUSE (*Page* 50)
The first verse can be said by the whole class in chorus. Verses two and three and the first line of verse four may be said by the teacher; line 2 of verse four can be taken by a student playing the part of a frog; line 1 of verse five may be said by the teacher and line 2 by a student who, throughout the poem, can speak the part of the mouse. Verses nine to twelve can be said by the teacher and verse thirteen by the whole class in chorus.
VOCABULARY
buckler: round shield.
e'en: even.

AT NIGHT (*Page* 52)
The two lines of the first verse can be spoken by a small group, or by a soloist. The whole of the second verse may be said by the teacher. In the

Poems to Enjoy, Book Three (5th edition)

third verse the first line and the first word of the second line can be spoken by the group, whilst the rest of the verse is said by a soloist. In verse four, the first line can be given to the group, the second line to a soloist, and the last two lines to the class in chorus.

SAMPAN (Page 53)
Good practice for initial and final consonants, particularly *p, t* and *f*. 'ae' (*a* as in 'sat') is also practised. The whole class can say the first four lines together, the teacher might speak lines 5-8 and four separate groups can take each of the lines, 9, 10, 11 and 12.

THE TOY BAND (*Page* 54)
In the first verse, lines 1 to 4 can be spoken by the teacher and lines 5 to 8, plus lines 1 to 3 and half of line 4 in the second verse, might be taken either by a soloist, or by a selected group. The second half of line 4 in verse two can be said by the teacher and lines 5 to 8 by a soloist, or by the group. Lines 1 to 4 in the third verse can be the teacher's, whilst lines 5 to 8 can again be taken by the soloist or by the group. In the last verse, the teacher might speak the first four lines, whilst the whole class in chorus says line 5 to 8.
VOCABULARY
dragoon: a cavalryman; a mounted soldier.

THE SPLENDOUR FALLS (*Page* 56)
At first, the teacher and then individual students can speak lines 1 to 4 in each verse of the poem. The last two lines of each verse can be taken by the whole class in chorus.
VOCABULARY
snowy summits: highest points, the snowy tops of the mountains.
cataract: waterfall.
scar: high, rocky part of a mountain.
glens: small, narrow valleys.

A FARMER HE LIVED (*Page* 57)
In verse one, lines 1, 3 and 4 can be the teacher's and lines 5 and 6 can be taken by a soloist; a similar arrangement being used in the second verse. In the third verse, one soloist may speak the first, third and fourth lines, and another soloist lines 5 and 6. Verse four can be treated similarly. The first, third and fourth lines of verse five can be the teacher's, whilst a soloist from the class speaks lines 5 and 6. The

Poems to Enjoy, Book Three (5th edition)

arrangement in the sixth verse can be similar. In verse seven, the treatment can be as for verses three and four and the last verse of the poem can be arranged as for the fifth verse.

The second line in each verse ('Bow down! Bow down!) may be spoken by the whole class in chorus.

VOCABULARY

gillyflower: another name for a wallflower; a scented flower.

PART TWO: PICTURES IN POETRY

FAIRYLAND (*Page* 60)
The class can be divided into three groups. Each group can be allocated one verse and the students in each group can be asked to sketch or paint what they 'see' when the poem is read to them by the teacher.

VOCABULARY

The barber in the story: may refer to "The Barber of Bagdad", whose stories are included in the famous story collection, "The Thousand and One Nights".

THE PALANQUIN BEARERS (*Page* 61)
A *palanquin* is a kind of chair or litter in which a person can be carried. If the students have not seen a picture of one, the teacher might make a sketch on the blackboard/whiteboard. This poem can be read by the teacher and class, for example, a small group *A* could read line 1; lines, 2, 3 and 4 could be spoken by three other groups, *B, C* and *D*; lines 5 and 6 by the first group *A* and line 7 by the whole class in chorus. Groups *B, C* and *D* could speak each of the lines 8, 9 and 10 separately, and the last two lines of the poem could then be read by the whole of the class in chorus. After the reading, the students may be asked to illustrate the poem.

THE DISMANTLED SHIP (*Page* 62)
After the teacher has read the poem to the class, sketching, painting and paper-cutting can be encouraged.

VOCABULARY

lagoon: a lake of salt-water separated from the sea by an atoll or sand-bank.

hawser'd: secured with hawsers or thick ropes.

Poems to Enjoy, Book Three (5th edition)

SILVER (*Page* 62)
After a reading by the teacher, a discussion and questions can follow. The teacher should try to make clear why the poet describes the trees, fruit, etc, as silver. (The light from the moon creates the effect).
VOCABULARY
shoon: old word for shoes.
casements: parts of windows, usually hinged.
cote: shelter for birds or animals.

ABOVE THE DOCK (*Page* 63)
This poem is for the students to illustrate after it has been read. Questions such as: 'Stand on the dockside with the poet and look up. What do you see?' Will help the students to understand this short poem. The poet is not trying to express an idea, but is trying to convey the feeling of a moonlit night at the docks. Students might find interesting the metaphorical comparison between the moon and a child's balloon.

THE PEDLAR OF SPELLS (*Page* 63)
Another vivid scene created in only five lines. After reading one or two other poems to the class to create a suitable atmosphere, the teacher might ask the students to sketch or paint the pedlar and his boy.
VOCABULARY
cranny: narrow hole or corner.

THE HORSEMAN (*Page* 63)
This poem, which refers to the effect of the moon's light, can be read in conjunction with the poems *Silver* and *Above the Dock*, both in Part Two. The scene described is very suitable for the class to illustrate.
VOCABULARY
helm: helmet.

THE HAWK (*Page* 64)
For illustration after a reading and discussion of the poem. Questions will help understanding, for example:
1. Why was the bird afraid?
2. What did the bird do when the hawk dived down?
3. Why would it have been better for the bird to have stayed where it was?
4. What happened to the bird after it fled?
5. Why was there 'no bird to sing'?

133

Poems to Enjoy, Book Three (5th edition)

THE EAGLE (*Page* 65)
For illustration.
VOCABULARY
crag: steep rock.
azure: skyblue in colour.

SNAIL (*Page* 65)
The teacher could, perhaps, bring a snail into the classroom to show to the students at the beginning of the lesson, before and after a first reading of the poem. This poem could also be introduced as part of a nature-study lesson.

THE VIPER (*Page* 66)
This poem could be used as an example before the students' own writing or sketching and painting on a similar theme. The snake each student depicts can be an inhabitant of his or her own country.
VOCABULARY
kestrel: a small hawk.
heath: a flat piece of waste land often covered by shrubs.
The fallen angel's comeliness: a reference to the Bible story. The fallen angel is Satan who was cast out from Heaven and, in the Garden of Eden, assumed the shape of a Serpent to tempt the first woman on earth, Eve.
comeliness: pleasant appearance.

THE SHIP (*Page* 67)
The teacher's reading can be followed by sketching and painting. The poet's comparison of the ship to a young doe, the use of the adjective 'snarling' and hyphenated 'tiger-foaming' can be discussed.
VOCABULARY
doe: a female deer or rabbit.
cat's paws: slight breezes.
snarling ocean: the ocean looks ill-tempered; in an angry mood.
tiger-foaming mouth: foaming at the mouth like a tiger.

THE WATERHEN (*Page* 67)
The four lines of this poem by D.G. Rossetti describe a scene which the class can be asked to illustrate. An accurate representation of the waterhen in flight should not, of course, be expected—it is the imaginative effort which counts.

Poems to Enjoy, Book Three (5th edition)

TO A BLACK GREYHOUND (*Page* 68)
The students can be divided into two groups after a preliminary reading. The first group can be asked to illustrate what they 'saw' after listening to the reading of the first verse, whilst the second group can be encouraged to illustrate verse two. Later the students can be asked to pick out the comparisons used by the poet and there might be some discussion of their meaning, such as:

Why does the poet described the greyhound as being:
1. 'Graceful as the swallow's flight'?
2. 'Swift as driven hurricane'?
3. 'Light as [a] swallow'?

CATS (*Page* 69)
After a first reading of this simple little poem, students can be asked to write their own poem about cats. Sketching and painting can also take place.

FROM PAPER BOATS (*Page* 70)
After the teacher's reading, a discussion and questions can follow:
1. What does the poet do 'day by day'?
2. What does he write on his paper boats?
3. What does he hope will happen to the boats?
4. With what does he load the boats?
5. What does he hope will happen to the flowers?

When the questions have been asked and the poem discussed, sketching and painting, or the making of paper boats, can begin, under the guidance of the teacher.

FLOOD (*Page* 70)
Useful as an example to read to the students, before they themselves begin writing on a similar theme. Alternatively, the students can be asked to sketch or paint what they imagine can be seen from the poet's 'eastern window'.

Poems to Enjoy, Book Three (5th edition)

AN OLD SONG RE-SUNG (*Page* 71)
This colourful poem is suitable for choral work and illustration. In each verse the whole class could speak lines 1, 2 and 5, whilst two soloists or two separate groups take lines 3 and 4. After two or three readings, the students could be asked to sketch or paint the scene suggested in one of the three verses.
VOCABULARY
bo'sun (boatswain): a ship's officer.
silver call: silver whistle.
brails: ropes on the edges of sails.

THE KRA (*Page* 72)
This poem is suitable for choral work and illustration. Lines 1, 2 and 3 can be spoken by three individuals or groups; lines 4 and 5 can be said by the whole class in chorus. Lines, 6, 7 and 8 might be taken by three groups, separately, and the whole class can speak the last line. Sketching and painting may then follow.
VOCABULARY
kra: a kind of monkey.

THE GALLANT SHIP (*Page* 72)
Lines 1, 2, 4 and 5 can be spoken by the teacher, and the whole class in chorus can read the third and sixth lines. This poem might be read together with the previous one. The scene lends itself to illustration.

A SPIKE OF GREEN (*Page* 73)
A simple little poem which can easily be illustrated after a reading by the teacher.

THE SHIP (*Page* 74)
Each verse of this poem is suitable for illustration.
VOCABULARY
pensive: deep in thought.

THE AEROPLANE (*Page* 75)
A simple poem which describes a suitable scene for illustration.

Poems to Enjoy, Book Three (5th edition)

COBWEBS (*Page* 76)
Before this poem is read, the students might be shown a cobweb and told something about the way the spider makes it. After the reading, sketching and painting can begin.
VOCABULARY
Myriad: a very large number.

THE RIVALS (*Page* 77)
The first, second, fifth and sixth lines of each verse of this poem can be spoken by the teacher, or by one of the students, or by a group. Lines 3 and 4 in each verse can be said by the whole class in chorus. The scene can be illustrated by the students after the readings.

THE TRAIN (*Page* 78)
For illustration by the students after the teacher has read the poem to them.
VOCABULARY
fain: wanting (the training carries away those who wish to stay).

WHITE HORSES (*Page* 79)
After the teacher's reading, the students can be allowed to sketch and paint what they 'see'.

THE CATERPILLAR (*Page* 80)
A simple poem which can be included in a nature-study lesson, or read in the poetry lesson before drawing and painting begins.

THE CLIFF-TOP (*Page* 80)
A simple poem for illustration after the teacher has read it aloud.

THE LITTLE DANCERS (*Page* 81)
After the teacher's first reading to the students, a discussion can follow. Some of the phraseology will need explanation, for instance: 'Into its gloom retires'; 'through an airy maze of motion lightly threaded with nimble feet'. Sketching and painting may follow the discussion.
VOCABULARY
secluded: away from people and things.
the dumb roar: the noise of traffic.
the brisk measure: fast rhythm.
sedately: free from hurry; composedly.

Poems to Enjoy, Book Three (5th edition)

PART THREE: A TALE IS TOLD

THE KING OF CHINA'S DAUGHTER (*Page* 84)
This highly imaginative tale of a fruitless courtship can be used to create 'atmosphere' before a lesson in which the students are to be encouraged to write their own poems. Too much time should not be taken up with explanations.

IN YUNG-YANG (*Page* 85
After the teacher's reading to the class, there can be a discussion and some questioning, for instance:
1. What does the poet remember when he returns to Yung-Yang?
2. What had happened to the poet's father's house?
3. How had the town changed?
4. What were still the same as before?
A final reading by the teacher may follow discussion.

THE SHIP OF RIO (*Page* 86)
After the teacher's reading to the class, there can be a discussion and some questioning, as follows:
1. Where did the ship come from?
2. Who were the crew? How many were there in the crew?
3. How did the crew move about the ship when reefing the sails?
4. Was the ship a motor-vessel, a steamship, or a sailing ship?
5. What did the crew do when the ship sailed to land?

This poem is written in sailor's language and the grammatical mistakes which appear (e.g. 'There weren't a stitch…'; 'There weren't one pair') are included deliberately by the poet to make it appear that the story is being told by a sailor, that is, to give the poem *realism*.
VOCABULARY
jovial: merry.
bo'sun: Ship's officer (boatswain)
caboose: a room for cooking on a ship's deck.
calico: material
to breech 'em: to put breeches/ trousers/jeans on them.
barnacle: a growth on the bottom of a ship.
shroud: one of the ropes supporting the mast of a ship.
reach-me-downs: trousers.
jabbering: chattering.

Poems to Enjoy, Book Three (5th edition)

gladsome: happy
reef her fore and aft: reducing the size of the sails in the front and rear of the ship.

LAST POEM (*Page* 87)
After a first reading by the teacher, the students can be asked to sketch and paint the scene described. When this work is finished, a number of the paintings and drawings can be shown to the class and discussed.
VOCABULARY
superintendence: arrangement of.

THE SNARE (*Page* 88)
A 'snare' is a trap, usually set to catch small animals. It is often made of a running noose of wire, rope or cord. The reading of this poem should be as effective as possible and explanations should be kept down to the minimum. After the reading, students can be asked to write their own stories and poems on a similar theme.

THE LOST SHOE (*Page* 89)
The teacher's first reading aloud can be followed by a discussion and some simple questions, for example:
1. What was Lucy doing when she lost her shoe?
2. Name two places in the house where Lucy looked for her shoe
3. Who did not 'breathe a whisper' of where the shoe had gone?
4. Why did Lucy hop whilst looking for her shoe?
5. Name three countries in which Lucy searched for her shoe.
A final reading can follow the discussion.
VOCABULARY
lamped: lit by many lamps.

OH! CRUEL WERE MY PARIENTS (*Page* 91)
In each verse of this poem, lines 1 to 4 could be said by four soloists or four groups, whilst the last line in each verse could be spoken by the whole class in chorus. A discussion might follow the reading. The Press Gang was a band of men whose job it was to forcibly recruit young men to serve in the army or navy. In the first verse, the story is told by Mary, but in the second verse the story is apparently taken up by the narrator.
VOCABULARY
parients: parents—the girl is speaking in dialect.
strand: beach.

Poems to Enjoy, Book Three (5th edition)

farden: farthing, a small English coin (*now obsolete*).

I KEEP SIX HONEST SERVING MEN (*Page* 92)
The class can join in the reading aloud of this poem after the teacher's introduction. In verse one, the teacher can speak the first, second, seventh, and eighth lines; the whole class can say lines 3 and 4 together; and lines 5 and 6 can be taken by two soloists, or by two different groups. The second verse can be spoken by the teacher, as can the first two lines of the third verse. The last two lines of the poem can be said by all the students in the class. The 'six honest serving-men' in Kipling's poem are, of course, the six words which usually introduce questions.

THE SEVEN FIDDLERS (*Page* 93)
A discussion and some questioning can follow two readings by the teachers, for example:
1. What did each of the fiddlers wear?
2. How many fiddlers were there?
3. What happened to people when the fiddlers played?
4. What did the fiddlers do when they arrived at the ferry at the side of the River Severn?
5. What two things did the fiddlers do when they arrived in mid-channel?
6. What happened to the ferry-boat after the fiddlers had stepped into the water?
7. How is it possible to know the place where the fiddlers walked into the water?
A final reading might follow the discussion.

The River Severn runs through the City of Worcester, in England.

SOLDIER, WON'T YOU MARRY ME? (*Page* 95)
The first three lines of verses one, three, five and seven can be spoken by the class in chorus, whilst the fourth line of each of these verses might be taken by a separate soloist. Verses two, four and six may be spoken by three different students or groups. After a second reading, the teachers can encourage a short discussion. Various questions can be asked and answered, for example:
1. What reasons does the soldier give for not marrying the girl?
2. What is the most important reason?

Poems to Enjoy, Book Three (5th edition)

3. What did the girl do each time the soldier gave a reason for not marrying her?
VOCABULARY
fife: a kind of small, high-pitched flute, used in military bands.

THE FISHER'S WIDOW (*Page* 97)
After two readings by the teacher, the students can be asked to sketch or paint what they 'see', or they can be encouraged to write their own stories or poems on the theme of the sailor who does not return after a voyage.
VOCABULARY
as the long days wane: as the days decline.

SONG FROM THE FLOWER OF OLD JAPAN (*Page* 98)
Alfred Noyes's long poem the *Flower of Old Japan* describes a colourful dream. The children fall asleep in their nursery after looking through some 'quaint old story-books' and dream of a journey to 'Old Japan'. Three different groups could read lines 1, 2, 3, 4, 5 and 6 in the first verse and the rest of the class, in chorus, could read the seventh and eighth lines. The teacher could speak the whole of the second verse himself or herself.
VOCABULARY
palanquin: see 'The Palanquin Bearers', above.
bowers: on land, a leafy nook; in the sea, a pleasant secluded place.

THE NIGHTJAR (*Page* 99)
A nightjar is a common bird which appears mainly at night. The male can be distinguished by the peculiar whirring sound it makes at certain times in the year. The bird is sometimes known as a goat-sucker. Explanations after the reading should be kept to the minimum at this stage.
VOCABULARY
full fathom five: right down to five fathoms. A fathom is a measure of depth (This a quotation from William Shakespeare's play, *The Tempest*, Act 1, Scene 2).

THE UPSIDE-DOWN WORLD (*Page* 100)
A simple little poem. "The place that holds the sky is", of course, a pond and the little girl who "nods and smiles" is the little girl telling the story, who is reflected in the pond.

141

Poems to Enjoy, Book Three (5th edition)

THE HAG (*Page* 101)
This poem can be illustrated by the students, or used as an example before the students are asked to write their own poems and stories about a witch. Before work of this kind begins, the poem can be read aloud by teacher and class. In each verse, the teacher might say the first, second, fourth and fifth lines, whilst the class, in chorus, speaks the third and sixth lines.
VOCABULARY
burr: a kind of thorn.
spur: a spike usually attached to the rider's heel to urge on a horse.
mires: swamps; marshes.

THE SILVER ROAD *(Page* 102)
'The Silver Road' is made from the reflection of the moon's light on the sea. This simple little poem can serve as an example to be read to the class before sketching and/or painting begin.

THE BALLAD OF EARL HALDAN'S DAUGHTER (*Page* 103)
The entire class can take part in the reading of this ballad. The teacher might speak the first four lines of verse one; one girl or boy can say lines 5 and 6, and the whole class can speak lines 7 and 8. In verse two, all the lines can be read by the teacher or by one good student-soloist, except for the last two lines which can again be taken by all the students in the class. Verse three can be said by a boy soloist and in verse four the teacher can speak lines 1 to 4; the boy soloist can take lines 5 and 6, whilst the last two lines of the poem may be said by the whole class.
VOCABULARY
ballad: a poem which tells a story. The verses are usually short and there is an easy, swinging rhythm throughout. Many ballads have been set to music.

TARTARY (*Page* 104)
When this poem has been read, there can be poetry and story-writing on the theme, 'If I were...'
VOCABULARY
flaunt: to "show off"
*athwar*t: across
bray: play loudly.
mandoline: A stringed musical instrument.
ere: before; *scimitar*: a curved sword.

142

Poems to Enjoy, Book Three (5th edition)

ELDORADO (*Page* 106)
'Eldorado' is a fictitious country, rich in gold and imagined as most desirable to live in.
The class can take part in the reading of this poem. The first two verses can be spoken by the teacher, except for the last two lines in each, which may be taken by the whole class in chorus. In verse three, the first three lines can be said by the teacher and the last three by a student soloist. The whole of verse four, except for line 5, which can be taken by the teacher, can be said by another student.
VOCABULARY
bedight: dressed.

THE LION (*Page* 107)
After a reading by the teacher, there can be a discussion and questions, for example:
1. Where is the lion?
2. What is the lion doing?
3. Is the lion afraid of 'the prying sons of men?'
4. Does the lion make a noise as he walks to and fro?
VOCABULARY
tawny: orange-brown colour.
ebb and flow: the movements of the lion's shoulder muscles are like the movement of the sea.
pads: treads silently.
flaming: leaping.

HIAWATHA'S CHILDHOOD (*Page* 108)
After the teacher has read this poem to the class, there can be a discussion and some questioning, for instance:
1. What was the fire-fly called?
2. Who had taught Hiawatha the song about the fire-fly?
3. How did the shadows come to be on the moon?
4. How is a rainbow formed?
VOCABULARY
brakes: thickets.
flecks: specks, patches of colour.

WANDER-THIRST (*Page* 110)
The teacher can speak most of the poem, the class saying the last line in each verse in chorus. A discussion can follow the reading.

Poems to Enjoy, Book Three (5th edition)

THE MINSTREL BOY (*Page* 111)
The dialogue in this poem can be spoken by an individual student whilst the teacher speaks the remainder. The poem is suitable to be used as an example before the student's own poetry and story-writing begin.
VOCABULARY
girded: fastened.
bard: a poet.
asunder: apart.
sully: soil; discredit.

THE EMPEROR OF CHINA (*Page* 112)
Four groups in this class can be given one verse each to illustrate, after the teacher has read the poem twice. A discussion and questions can then follow, for example:
1. What was the emperor's throne made of?
2. What did he decide to have for dinner?
3. Where was the nightingale?
4. What happened to the nightingale?
5. Why didn't the Emperor finish his meal?
VOCABULARY
canopied: covered with.
pouted: thrust out his lips.
savours: tastes.
languidly: without energy, vitality.
dells: wooded hollows.

DOWN OUR STREET (*Page* 114)
The teacher's reading may be followed by a discussion and questions, as follows:
1. What did the man do when he met the boy?
2. What did the boy think he saw?
3. Why did the boy believe himself to be stupid and slow?

This poem refers to the mysterious power of the imagination. It is unlikely that it will be fully understood by the students but it can be enjoyed, nevertheless. It might be advisable, after the first reading, for the teacher to deal with each verse in turn.
VOCABULARY
hyaline: as clear as crystal.

Poems to Enjoy, Book Three (5th edition)

MILK FOR THE CAT (*Page* 115)
The teacher can read the poem twice to the class. A discussion may then begin and the teacher can stimulate this by acting suitable questions, such as:
1. At what time is the tea brought?
2. For what purpose does the cat pretend to have come in?
3. What is the cat's real purpose?
4. Why does the cat's appearance change?
5. Where does the saucer come from?
6. What does the cat do after she has drunk the milk?
A final reading can follow the discussion.
VOCABULARY
agate: precious stone.
lust: a great desire.
transfigured: changed in aspect.
ecstasy: rapturous, very pleasurable feeling.

UP AND AWAY (*Page* 117)
After the teacher has first read the poem, each of the students can be asked to sketch or paint their own district as they imagine it might look from a low-flying aeroplane. A discussion and questions can follow, such as:
1. By what means does the author want to travel to France or Spain?
2. What do the fields look like from an aeroplane?
3. What is the 'big letter T'?
4. How does the pilot receive the news?
5. Why is the aeroplane 'like a bird coming home' when it arrives at the aerodrome (airport)?
A final reading can conclude the lesson.

TWO RED ROSES ACROSS THE MOON (*Page* 119)
This poem is a *ballad*. (See explanation given in the note to 'The Ballad Of Earl Haldan's Daughter', above.). For the reading, the class can be divided into two halves. Each half can take turns to speak the refrain, 'Two red roses across the moon', in chorus, whilst the remainder of each verse is spoken either by the teacher or a number of soloists chosen from among the students.
A discussion of the story can follow and questions, such as those over the page, will help the students to understand the poem:

Poems to Enjoy, Book Three (5th edition)

1. Why didn't the knight stop when he heard the lady's song?
2. For how long did the knight ride 'on the spur'?
3. What did the knight say to himself just before noon?
4. What did the knight do when he returned from the battle?
5. What helped the knight's army to win the battle?
6. How did the knight show the lady that he was grateful?

A final reading can complete the lesson.
VOCABULARY
forsooth: to be sure; it is certain.
may: hawthorn blossom.
rode on the spur: he urged on the horse.
trow: hope, believe, swear

BOOT AND SADDLE (*Page* 121)
As the teacher speaks this poem, all the class can say the refrain, 'Boot, saddle, to horse and away!' each time it occurs, After the reading, the students can be asked to write stories of their own about a siege and the relief of a castle or a town.
VOCABULARY
strike up the lay: sing the line or song.
roebuck: small deer.

Poems to Enjoy, Book Three (5th edition)

Poems to Enjoy, Book Three (5th edition)

ABOUT THE EDITOR

Verner Bickley is an educationist who has led international education projects in Singapore, Burma, Indonesia, Japan, Saudi Arabia and Hong Kong. For two years, he was Chairman of Directors of the East-West Centre in Hawaii and, for ten years, was Director of the Centre's Culture Learning Institute. He has served as an adjudicator in speech and drama festivals in several countries and as President of the English-Speaking Union in Hawaii and Chairman of the English-Speaking Union in Hong Kong. He has lived and worked in Hong Kong since 1983.

Specialising in institutional linguistics, language pedagogy and international education, Dr Bickley has written extensively on language and culture and on language learning and teaching. He has served as announcer and actor in radio and TV programmes broadcast in several Asian and Pacific countries. His voice was heard regularly over the NHK in Tokyo, the Burma Broadcasting Service, Radio Republic Indonesia and Radio Malaya where he broadcast from Singapore as newsreader and as actor and narrator in radio drama, as well as in programmes for schools and colleges.

Among the dozens of scripts he has written were five in a series on the use of poetry in the language class, broadcast in BBC radio's "Listen and Teach" series. Twenty scripts written by Dr Bickley for the Japan Broadcasting Company were broadcast as the television series, "How English Works".

His books include *Reading and Interpretation* (co-authored), *Reading and Understanding* (co-authored), *A New Malayan Songbook* (co-authored), *Easy English*, *Cultural Relations in the Global Community*, *Searching for Frederick* (an autobiographical-biographical narrative), *Language and the Young Learner in Hong Kong*, and *Forward to Beijing*. The first volume of his autobiography entitled, *Footfalls Echo in the Memory*, was published in 2010 and the second volume, *Steps to Paradise and Beyond: Hawaii to China, Saudi Arabia, Hong Kong and Elsewhere*, in 2013.

Born in Cheshire, England, Dr Bickley received two bachelor's degrees from the University of Wales, before earning an M.A. degree in education there. He was made a Licentiate of the Royal

149

Poems to Enjoy, Book Three (5th edition)

Aademy of Music (Speech and Drama) in 1955 and a Licentiate of the Guildhall School of Music and Drama in the same year. He was awarded a PhD in socio-linguistics by the University of London in 1966. He is a Fellow of the Royal Society of Arts.

Employed by the British Council for twelve years, he moved from university teaching and advisory assignments to the position of English Language Officer for Japan and First Secretary in the Cultural Department of the British Embassy in Tokyo.

Dr Bickley was founding Director of the Hong Kong Government's Institute of Language in Education (which was incorporated into the Hong Kong Institute of Education after his retirement) and an Assistant Director of Education.

Dr Bickley was made a Member of the Order of the British Empire in 1964.

Poems to Enjoy, Book Three (5th edition)

ABOUT PROVERSE HONG KONG

Proverse Hong Kong, co-founded by Gillian and Verner Bickley, is based in Hong Kong, with growing regional and international connections.

Verner Bickley has headed cultural and educational centres, departments, institutions and projects in many parts of the world. Gillian Bickley has recently concluded a career as a university teacher of English Literature, spanning four continents. Proverse Hong Kong draws on their combined academic, administrative and teaching experience as well as varied long-term participation in reading, research, writing, editing, reviewing, publishing and authorship.

Proverse Hong Kong has published novels, novellas, single author short story collections, non-fiction (including memoirs, biography, war and travel diaries and journals, fictionalised autobiography, history, sport), single-author poetry collections, editions of nineteenth-century writing, academic and young teen books. Other interests include academic works in the humanities, social sciences, cultural studies, linguistics and education. Some Proverse books have accompanying audio texts. Proverse editors work with texts by non-native-speaker writers of English as well as by native English-speaking writers.

Proverse welcomes authors who have a story to tell, wisdom, perceptions or information to convey, a person they want to memorialise, a neglect they want to remedy, a record they want to correct, a strong interest which they want to share, skills they want to teach, and who consciously seek to make a contribution to society in an informative, interesting and well-written way.

The name, *Proverse*, combines the words "prose" and "verse" and is pronounced accordingly.

Poems to Enjoy, Book Three (5th edition)

SOME EDUCATIONAL BOOKS FROM PROVERSE

Jockey, by Gillian Bickley (when Gillian Workman). Hong Kong, 1979. Pbk. 64pp. ISBN-10: 962-85570-3-3; ISBN-13: 978-962-85570-3-5.

Poems to Enjoy: Book 1, Edited by Verner Bickley. HK & UK: 2012. Pbk. 136 pp. (inc. 35 b/w original line-drawings & Teacher's and Student's Notes). With audio CDs. ISBN 978-988-8167-54-8.

Poems to Enjoy: Book 2, Edited by Verner Bickley. HK & UK: 2013. Pbk. 136pp. (inc. 37 b/w original line-drawings & Teacher's and Student's Notes). With audio CDs. ISBN 978-988-8167-51-7.

Poems to Enjoy: Book 3, Edited by Verner Bickley. HK & UK: 2013. Pbk. 166 pp. (inc. 39 b/w original line-drawings & Teacher's and Student's Notes). w. audio CDs. ISBN 978-988-19934-1-0.

Poems to Enjoy: Book 4, Edited by Verner Bickley. HK & UK: scheduled, 2014. Pbk. *c.*174 pp. (inc. *c.*41 b/w original line-drawings & Teacher's and Student's Notes). With audio CDs. ISBN 978-988-8167-50-0.

Poems to Enjoy: Book 5, Edited by Verner Bickley. HK & UK: scheduled, 2015. Pbk. *c.*200 pp. (inc. *c.*36 b/w original line-drawings & Teacher's and Student's Notes). With audio CD(s) / DVD(s). ISBN 978-988-8167-49-4.

Spanking Goals and Toe Pokes: Football Sayings Explained, by T. J. Martin. HK & UK, 2008. ISBN-13: 978-988-99668-2-9.

Teachers' and Students' Guide to the Book and Audio Book, 'The Golden Needle: the Biography of Frederick Stewart (1836-1889)'. Proverse Hong Kong Study Guides. E-book. ISBN-10: 962-85570-9-2; ISBN-13: 978-962-85570-9-7. 24Reader e-book edition (2010), ISBN-13: 978-988-19320-5-1.

Poems to Enjoy, Book Three (5th edition)

THE PROVERSE INTERNATIONAL LITERARY PRIZES

THE INTERNATIONAL PROVERSE PRIZE

The Proverse Prize, an annual international competition for an unpublished single-author book-length work of fiction, non-fiction, or poetry, the original work of the entrant, submitted in English (translations are welcome) was established in January 2008. It is open to all who are at least eighteen on the date they sign the entry form and without restriction of nationality, residence or citizenship.

The objectives of the prize are: to encourage excellence and / or excellence and usefulness in publishable written work in the English Language, which can, in varying degrees, "delight and instruct". Entries are invited from anywhere in the world.

Entry forms available each year from	No later than 14 April
Closing date for entry forms, fees and entered work	30 June
Judging	July-September
Semi-finalists announced	No later than November

THE INTERNATIONAL PROVERSE POETRY PRIZE (SINGLE POEMS)

Entry forms, entry fees, and entered work received from	7 May
Closing date for entry forms, fees and entered work	30 June
Judging	July-September
Winners announced	No later than November

More information, updated from time to time, is available on the Proverse Hong Kong website: proversepublishing.com

FIND OUT MORE ABOUT PROVERSE AUTHORS BOOKS AND EVENTS

Visit our website:
http://www.proversepublishing.com
Visit our distributor's website: www.chineseupress.com

Follow us on Twitter
Follow news and conversation: <twitter.com/Proversebooks>
OR
Copy and paste the following to your browser window and follow the instructions:
https://twitter.com/#!/ProverseBooks

"Like" us on www.facebook.com/ProversePress
Request our free E-Newsletter
Send your request to info@proversepublishing.com.

Availability

Most books are available in Hong Kong and world-wide from our Hong Kong based Distributor,
The Chinese University Press of Hong Kong,
The Chinese University of Hong Kong, Shatin, NT,
Hong Kong SAR, China.
Email: cup-bus@cuhk.edu.hk
Website: www.chineseupress.com

All titles are available from Proverse Hong Kong
http://www.proversepublishing.com
and the Proverse Hong Kong UK-based Distributor.

We have stock-holding retailers in Hong Kong,
Canada (Elizabeth Campbell Books),
Andorra (Llibreria La Puça, La Llibreria).
Orders can be made from bookshops
in the UK and elsewhere.

Ebooks
Most of our titles are available also as Ebooks

www.ingramcontent.com/pod-product-compliance
Lightning Source LLC
Chambersburg PA
CBHW070049100426
42734CB00040B/2817